THE MOST FAMOUS BOOK IN AMERICA ON THE RELATIONS BE- TWEEN PARENTS AND THEIR CHILDREN!

OVER 60 WEEKS ON THE BESTSELLER LIST!

"Simply stated, with specific words and ideas that parents can use in child guidance . . . Combines good science with good common sense."

Family Life

"The presentation is direct, fresh, and easy to understand. Advice is supported by illustrative dialogue and anecdotes. The reader will sense that the author is an effective teacher; his suggested conversations with children are contagious—one easily picks up his method of talking with children.

Reading this book will be rewarding not only to parents but also to everyone who must 'relate' to children. Having read it once, you will not want to discard it, but rather keep it as a handy reference for life situations."

Christian Home and School

"A helpful, important book by an expert in child psychology and parent guidance."

Together

"Time and again one comes on observations so true and so well put that there is an urge to copy them and hang them over the kitchen sink."

The Episcopalian

"Parents have been studying children-ese and putting it into practice. All those we interviewed found the method . . . infinitely rewarding."

The New York Times

"Dozens of extremely helpful ideas for achieving those goals which most parents hold . . . it is a great relief to hear from enlightened professionals who have practical, illustrated advice."

Christian Science Monitor

Between Parent &Child

New solutions to old problems

Dr. Haim G. Ginott

NEW YORK UNIVERSITY

AN AVON BOOK

AVON BOOKS
A division of
The Hearst Corporation
959 Eighth Avenue
New York, New York 10019

First Avon Printing, March, 1969

Cover illustration by

AVON TRADEMARK REG. U.S. PAT. OFF. AND
FOREIGN COUNTRIES, REGISTERED TRADEMARK—
MARCA REGISTRADA, HECHO EN CHICAGO, U.S.A.

Printed in the U.S.A.

Acknowledgment is gratefully made to the following
copyright holders for permission to reprint from
previously published materials:

McGraw-Hill Book Company for an exerpt from
Group Psychotherapy with Children by Dr. Haim G.
Ginott. Copyright © 1961 Haim G. Ginott. Used by
permission of McGraw-Hill Book Company.

The Viking Press Inc. for an excerpt from *East of Eden*
by John Steinbeck. Copyright 1952.

Harper and Row for an excerpt from *Child
Behavior* by Francis L. Ilg and Louis B. Ames.
Copyright 1955.

To the memory of my younger brother

Contents

Contents

Contents

Preface

No parent wakes up in the morning planning to make his child's life miserable. No mother says to herself, "Today I'll yell, nag, and humiliate my child whenever possible." On the contrary. In the morning many mothers resolve: "This is going to be a peaceful day. No yelling, no arguing, and no fighting." Yet, in spite of good intentions, the unwanted war breaks out again. Once more we find ourselves saying things we do not mean, in a tone we do not like.

All parents want their children to be secure and happy. No one deliberately tries to make his child fearful, shy, inconsiderate, or obnoxious. Yet in the process of growing up, many children acquire undesirable characteristics and fail to achieve a sense of security and an attitude of respect for themselves and for others. We want children to be polite and they are rude; we want them to be neat and they are messy; we want them to be self-confident and they are insecure; we want them to be happy and they are not.

The purpose of this book is to help parents identify their goals in relation to children and to suggest methods of achieving those goals. Parents are confronted with concrete problems that require specific solutions; they are not helped by cliché advice such as "Give the child more love," "Show him more attention," "Offer him more time."

For the last fifteen years, the author has worked with parents and children in individual, as well as in group, guidance and psychotherapy. The book is the fruit of this experience. It is a practical guide: it offers concrete suggestions and preferred solutions for dealing with daily situations and psychological problems faced by all parents. While the book gives specific advice, it also sets forth basic principles to guide parents in living with children in mutual respect and dignity.

Acknowledgments

I am grateful to my friends and colleagues who read the manuscript and contributed suggestions and criticism: Dr. Ralph Dreger, Sue Zohar Desheh, Bea Livingston, Dr. Arthur Orgel, Patricia and Howard Pearl, Angela Podkameni and Rosalind Wiener. Special thanks to Bette Kaufman for assistance and encouragement, and to Dr. Stanley Spiegel for his help in starting the book. Lastly, to the parents who shared with me their feelings and experience, I acknowledge my greatest debt.

HAIM G. GINOTT

Between Parent & Child

New solutions to old problems

CHAPTER 1

Conversing
with children

CHILDREN'S QUESTIONS: THE HIDDEN MEANINGS

Conversing with children is a unique art with rules and meanings of its own. Children are rarely naive in their communications. Their messages are often in a code, that requires deciphering.

Andy, age ten, asked his father, "What is the number of abandoned children in Harlem?"

Father, a chemist and an intellectual, was glad to see his son take an interest in social problems. He gave a long lecture on the subject and then looked up the figure. But Andy was not satisfied and kept on asking questions on the same subject: "What is the number of abandoned children in New York City?" "in the United States?" "in Europe?" "in the world?"

Finally it occurred to father that his son was concerned, not about a social problem, but by a personal one. His questions stemmed not so much from sympathy for abandoned children as from fear of being abandoned. He was looking, not for a figure representing the number of deserted children, but for reassurance that he would not be deserted.

On his first visit to kindergarten, while mother was still with him, Bruce, age five, looked over the paintings on the wall and asked loudly, "Who made these ugly pictures?"

Mother was embarrassed. She looked at her son disapprovingly, and hastened to tell him, "It's not nice to call the pictures ugly when they are so pretty."

The teacher, who understood the meaning of the question, smiled and said, "In here you don't have to paint pretty pictures. You can paint mean pictures if you feel like it." A big smile appeared on Bruce's face, for now he had the answer to his hidden question: "What happens to a boy who doesn't paint so well?"

Next Bruce picked up a broken fire engine and asked self-righteously, "Who broke this fire engine?" Mother answered, "What difference does it make to you who broke it? You don't know anyone here."

Bruce was not really interested in names. He wanted to find out what happened to boys who break toys. Understanding the question, the teacher gave an appropriate answer: "Toys are for playing. Sometimes they get broken. It happens."

Bruce seemed satisfied. His interviewing skill had netted him the necessary information:

"This grownup is pretty nice. She does not get angry quickly, even when a picture comes out ugly or a toy is broken. I don't have to be afraid. It is safe to stay here." Bruce waved good-by to his mother and went over to the teacher to start his first day in kindergarten.

Carol, age twelve, was tense and tearful. Her favorite cousin was going home after staying with her during the summer.

CAROL (*with tears in her eyes*): Susie is going away. I'll be all alone again.

MOTHER: You'll find another friend.

CAROL: I'll be so lonely.

MOTHER: You'll get over it.

CAROL: Oh, mother! (*Sobs.*)

MOTHER: You are twelve years old and still such a crybaby.

Carol gave mother a deadly look and escaped to her room, closing the door behind her.

This episode should have had a happier ending. A child's feeling must be taken seriously, even though the situation itself is not very serious. In mother's eyes a summer separation may be too minor a crisis for tears, but her response need not have lacked sympathy. Mother might have said to herself, "Carol is distressed. I can help her best by showing that I understand what pains her." To her daughter she might have said any or all of the following:

"It will be lonely without Susie."

"You miss her already."

"It is hard to be apart when you are so used to being together."

"The house must seem kind of empty to you without Susie around."

Such responses create intimacy between parent and child. When the child feels understood, his loneliness and hurt diminish, because they are understood, and his love for mother is deepened because she understands. Mother's sympathy serves as an emotional band-aid for the bruised ego.

FRUITLESS DIALOGUES

Parents are frustrated by dialogues with children because they lead nowhere, as illustrated by the famous conversation: "Where did you go?" "Out." "What did you do?" "Nothing." Parents who try to be reasonable soon discover how exhausting this can be. As one mother said, "I try to reason with my child until I am blue in the face, but he doesn't listen to me. He only hears me when I scream."

Children often resist dialogues with parents. They resent being preached to, talked at, and criticized. They feel that parents talk too much. Says eight-year-old David to his mother, "When I ask you a small question, why do you give me such a long answer?" To his friends he confides, "I don't tell mother anything. If I start in with her, I have no time left to play."

An interested observer who overhears a conversation between a parent and a child will note with surprise how little each listens to the other. The conversation sounds like two monologues, one consisting of criticism and instructions, the other of denials and pleading. The tragedy of such "communication" lies, not in the lack of love, but in the lack of respect; not in the lack of intelligence, but in the lack of skill.

Our everyday language is not adequate for communicating meaningfully with children. To reach children and to reduce parental frustration, we need a new mode of relating to children, including new ways of conversing with them.

THE NEW CODE OF COMMUNICATION

The new code of communication with children is based on respect and on skill. It requires (*a*) that messages preserve the child's as well as the parent's self-respect; (*b*) that statements of understanding *precede* statements of advice or instruction.

Eric, age nine, came home full of anger. His class was scheduled to go for a picnic, but it was raining. Mother decided to use a new approach. She refrained from clichés that in the past had only made things worse: "There is no use crying over rained-out picnics." "There will be other days for fun." "I didn't make it rain, you know, so why are you angry at me?"

To herself she said, "My son has strong feelings about missing the picnic. He is disappointed. He is sharing his disappointment with me by showing me his anger. He is entitled to his emotions. I can best help him by showing understanding and respect for his feelings." To Eric she said:

MOTHER: You seem very disappointed.

ERIC: Yes.

MOTHER: You wanted very much to go to this picnic.

ERIC: I sure did.

MOTHER: You had everything ready and then the darn rain came.

ERIC: Yes, that's exactly right.

There was a moment of silence and then Eric said, "Oh, well, there will be other days."

His anger seemed to have vanished and he was quite cooperative the rest of the afternoon. Usually when Eric came home angry, the whole household would be upset. Sooner or later he provoked every member of the family. Peace would not return until he was finally asleep late in the evening.

What is so special about this approach, and what are its helpful components?

When a child is in the midst of strong emotions, he cannot listen to anyone. He cannot accept advice or consolation or constructive criticism. He wants *us* to understand him. He wants us to understand what is going on inside himself at that particular moment. Furthermore, he wants to be understood without having to disclose fully what he is experiencing. It is a game in which he reveals only a little of what he feels needing to have us guess the rest.

When a child tells us, "The teacher spanked me," we do not have to ask him for more details. Nor do we need to say, "What did you do to deserve it? If your teacher spanked you, you must have done something. What did you do?" We don't even have to say, "Oh, I am so sorry." We need to show him that we understand his pain and embarrassment and feelings of revenge. How do we know what he feels? We look at him and listen to him, and we also draw on our own emotional experiences. We know what a child *must* feel when he is shamed in public in the presence of peers. We so phrase our words that the child knows we understand what he has gone through. Any of the following statements would serve well:

"It must have been terribly embarrassing."

"It must have made you furious."

"You must have hated the teacher at that moment."

"It must have hurt your feelings terribly."

"It was a bad day for you."

A child's strong feelings do not disappear when he is told, "It is not nice to feel that way," or when the parent tries to convince him that he "has no reason to feel that way." Strong feelings do not vanish by being banished; they do diminish in intensity and lose their sharp edges when the listener accepts them with sympathy and understanding.

This statement holds true not only for children but also for adults, as illustrated by the following excerpt* from a parents' discussion group:

LEADER: Suppose it is one of those mornings when everything seems to go wrong. The telephone rings, the baby cries, and before you know it, the toast is burnt. Your husband looks over the toaster and says: "My God! When will you learn to make toast?!" What is your reaction?

MRS. A: I would throw the toast in his face!

MRS. B: I would say, "Fix your own damn toast!"

MRS. C: I would be so hurt I could only cry.

LEADER: What would your husband's words make you feel toward him?

PARENTS: Anger, hate, resentment.

LEADER: Would it be easy for you to fix another batch of toast?

MRS. A: Only if I could put some poison in it!

LEADER: And when he left for work, would it be easy to clean up the house?

MRS. A: No, the whole day would be ruined.

LEADER: Suppose that the situation is the same: the toast is burnt but your husband, looking over the situation, says, "Gee, honey, it's a rough morning for you—the baby, the phone, and now the toast."

* Haim G. Ginott, *Group Psychotherapy With Children* (New York: McGraw-Hill Book Co., 1961), pp. 180-182.

MRS. A: I would drop dead if my husband said that to me!

MRS. B: I would feel wonderful!

MRS. C: I would feel so good I would hug him and kiss him.

LEADER: Why?—that baby is still crying and the toast is still burnt?

PARENTS: That wouldn't matter.

LEADER: What would make the difference?

MRS. B: You feel kind of grateful that he didn't criticize you—that he was with you, not against you.

LEADER: And when your husband left for work, would it be difficult to clean up the house?

MRS. C: No! I'd do it with a song.

LEADER: Let me now tell you about a third kind of husband. He looks over the burnt toast and says to you calmly, "Let me show you, honey, how to make toast."

MRS. A: Oh, no. He is even worse than the first one. He makes you feel stupid.

LEADER: Let's see how these three different approaches to the toast incident apply to our handling of children.

MRS. A: I see what you're driving at. I always say to my child, "You are old enough to know this, you are old enough to know that." It must make him furious. It usually does.

MRS. B: I always say to my son, "Let me show you, dear, how to do this or that."

MRS. C: I'm so used to being criticized that it comes natural to me. I use exactly the same

words my mother used *against* me when I
was a child. And I hated her for it. I never
did anything right, and she always made me
do things over.

LEADER: And you now find yourself using the
same words with your daughter?

MRS. C: Yes. I don't like it at all—I don't like
myself when I do it.

LEADER: You are looking for better ways of
talking with your children.

MRS. C: Yes, I sure am!

LEADER: Let's see what we can learn from the
burnt toast story. What is it that helped
change the mean feelings to loving ones?

MRS. B: The fact that somebody understood you.

MRS. C: Without blaming you.

MRS. A: And without telling you how to im-
prove.

This vignette illustrates the power of words
to engender hostility or happiness. The moral of
the story is that our responses (words and feelings) can make a decided difference in the atmosphere of our home.

SOME PRINCIPLES OF CONVERSATION

From event to relationship.—When a child
tells of, or asks about, an event, it is frequently
best to respond, not to the event, but to the
relationship implied.

Flora, age six, complained that "lately" she

had been receiving fewer presents than her brother. Mother did not deny the complaint. Neither did she explain that brother was older and so deserved more. Nor did she promise to right the wrong. She knew that children are more concerned about the depth of their relationships with parents than about the size and number of gifts. Mother said, "You, too, want more presents?" Without adding another sentence, mother embraced her daughter, who responded with a smile of surprise and pleasure. This was the end of a conversation that could have become an endless argument.

From event to feelings.—When a child tells of an event, it is sometimes helpful to respond, not to the event itself, but to the feelings around it. Gloria, age seven, came home upset. She told mother how her girl friend Dori was pushed off the sidewalk into a rain-filled gutter. Instead of asking for more details of the event, mother responded to her daughter's feelings. She said:

"That must have upset you."

"You were angry at the boys who did it."

"You are still mad at them."

To all these statements, Gloria responded with an emphatic "Yes!" When mother said, "You are afraid that they may do it to you, too?"—Gloria answered with determination, "Let them try, I'll drag them with me. That would make a splash!" And she started to laugh at the picture in her mind of the drag and splash. This was the happy ending of a conver-

Conversing with children

sation that could have become a sermon of useless advice on methods of self-defense.

When a child comes home with a host of complaints about a friend or a teacher or about his
life, it is best to respond to his feeling tone,
instead of trying to ascertain facts or to verify
incidents.

Ten-year-old Harold came home cranky and
complaining.

HAROLD: What a miserable life! The teacher
called me a liar, just because I told her that I
forgot the homework. And she yelled. My
goodness, did she yell! She said she'll write
you a note.

MOTHER: You had a very rough day.

HAROLD: You can say that again.

MOTHER: It must have been terribly embarrassing to be called a liar in front of the whole
class.

HAROLD: It sure was.

MOTHER: I bet inside yourself you wished her a
few things!

HAROLD: Oh, yes! But how did you know?

MOTHER: That's what we usually do when
someone hurts us.

HAROLD: That's a relief.

From general to specific.—When a child
makes a statement about himself, it is often
desirable to respond, not with agreement or
disagreement, but with details that convey to
the child an understanding beyond expectation.

When a child says, "I am not good in arith-

32

metic," it is of little help to tell him, "Yes, you are pretty lousy with figures." Nor is it helpful to dispute his opinion or to offer him cheap advice: "If you studied more, you would be better." Such hasty help only hurts his self-respect and the instant lesson only decreases his confidence.

His statement, "I am not good in arithmetic," can be met with earnestness and understanding. Any of the following would do:

"Arithmetic is not an easy subject."

"Some of the problems are very hard to figure out."

"The teacher does not make it easier with his criticism."

"He makes you feel stupid."

"I bet you can't wait for the hour to pass."

"When it is over, you feel safer."

"Exam time must be extra tough."

"You must be worrying a lot about failing."

". . . worrying about what we will think."

". . . afraid we'll be disappointed in you."

"We know some subjects are not easy."

"We have faith that you'll do your best."

A twelve-year-old boy related that he almost "dropped dead" when father talked to him with such understanding after he brought home a failing report card. His inner reaction was: "I must live up to my father's faith in me."

Once in a blue moon, almost every parent hears his son or daughter declare, "I am stupid." Knowing that *his* child cannot be stupid,

33

the parent sets out to convince him that he is bright.

SON: I am stupid.

FATHER: You are not stupid.

SON: Yes, I am.

FATHER: You are not. Remember how smart you were at camp? The counselor thought you were one of the brightest.

SON: How do you know what he thought?

FATHER: He told me so.

SON: Yah, how come he called me stupe all the time?

FATHER: He was just kidding.

SON: I am stupid, and I know it. Look at my grades in school.

FATHER: You just have to work harder.

SON: I already work harder and it doesn't help. I have no brains.

FATHER: You are smart, I know.

SON: I am stupid, *I* know.

FATHER (*loudly*): You are not stupid!

SON: Yes I am!

FATHER: You are not stupid, Stupid!

When a child declares that he is stupid or ugly or bad, nothing that we can say or do will change his self-image immediately. A person's ingrained opinion of himself resists direct attempts at alteration. As one child said to his father, "I know you mean well, Dad, but I am not *that* stupid to take your word that I am bright."

When a child expresses a negative view of himself, our denials and protests are of little help to him. They only bring forth a stronger declaration of his convictions. The best help we can offer is to show him that we understand not only his general feeling, but its implications:

SON: I am stupid.

FATHER (*seriously*): You really feel that way, don't you? You don't think of yourself as smart?

SON: No.

FATHER: Then you suffer inside quite a lot?

SON: Yeah.

FATHER: In school, you must be afraid a great deal of the time

... afraid you'll fail.

... afraid you'll get low marks.

When the teacher calls on you, you get confused.

Even when you know the answer, it doesn't come out right.

You are afraid that your words will sound ridiculous

... and that the teacher will criticize you.

... and that the children will laugh at you. So, many times you prefer to say nothing. I guess you can remember times when you said something and they laughed at you. It made you feel stupid in your own eyes. Hurt and angry, too. (Here the child may tell you of some of his experience.)

FATHER: Look, son! In my eyes you are a fine person. But you have a different opinion of yourself.

This conversation may not change the child's

image of himself right then and there, but it may plant in him a seed of doubt about his inadequacy. He may think to himself, "If my father understands me and considers me a fine person, perhaps I am not that worthless." The intimacy that such a conversation creates may lead the son to try to live up to his father's faith in him.

When a child says, "I never have good luck," no argument or explanation will change his belief. For every instance of good fortune that we mention, he will respond with two tales of misfortune. All we can do is to show him how intimately we understand the feelings that lead him to his belief:

SON: I never have good luck.

MOTHER: You really feel that way?

SON: Yes.

MOTHER: So when you play a game you think inside yourself, "I'm not going to win. I don't have luck."

SON: Yes, that's exactly what I think.

MOTHER: In school, if you know the answer you think, "Today the teacher is not going to call me."

SON: Yes.

MOTHER: But if you didn't do the homework, you think, "Today she *is* going to call on me."

SON: Yes.

MOTHER: I guess you can give me many more examples.

SON: Sure ... like for instance (*child gives examples*).

MOTHER: I am interested in what you think about luck. If something happens that you think is bad luck, or even good luck, come and tell me and we'll talk about it.

This conversation may not change the child's belief in his bad luck. It may, however, convey to him how lucky he is to have such an understanding mother.

VOICING OF AMBIVALENCE

Children love and resent us at the same time. They feel two ways about parents, teachers, and all persons who have authority over them. Parents find it difficult to accept ambivalence as a fact of life. They do not like it in themselves and cannot tolerate it in their children. They think that there is something inherently wrong in feeling two ways about people, especially about members of the family.

We can learn to accept the existence of ambivalent feelings in ourselves and in our children. To avoid unnecessary conflicts, children need to know that such feelings are normal and natural. We can spare a child much guilt and anxiety by acknowledging and voicing his ambivalent feelings:

"You seem to feel two ways about your teacher: you like him and you dislike him."

"You seem to have two feelings about your older brother: you admire him, but you also resent him."

"You have two thoughts on the subject; you would like to go to camp, but you also want to stay home."

A calm, noncritical statement of their ambivalence is helpful to children because it conveys to them that even their "mixed-up" feelings are not beyond comprehension. As one child said, "If my mixed-up feelings can be understood, they are not so mixed up." On the other hand, statements such as the following are definitely not helpful:

"Boy, are you mixed up! One minute you like your friend, then you resent him. Make up your mind, if you have one."

A sophisticated view of human reality takes account of the possibility that where there is love, there is also some hate; where there is admiration, there is also some envy; where there is devotion, there is also some hostility; where there is success, there is also apprehension. It takes great wisdom to realize that all feelings are legitimate: the positive, the negative, and the ambivalent.

It is not easy to accept such concepts inwardly. Our childhood training and adult education predispose us to a contrary view. We have been taught that negative feelings are "bad" and should not be felt or that we should be ashamed of them. The new and scientific approach states that only real acts can be judged

as "bad" or "good," imaginary acts cannot be.
Only conduct can be condemned or commend-
ed, feelings cannot and should not be. Judgment of feelings and censure of fantasy would
do violence both to political freedom and to
mental health.

Emotions are part of our genetic heritage.
Fish swim, birds fly, and people feel. Sometimes
we are happy, sometimes we are not; but sometimes in our life we are sure to feel anger and
fear, sadness and joy, greed and guilt, lust and
scorn, delight and disgust. While we are not
free to choose the emotions that arise in us, we
are free to choose how and when to express
them, provided we know what they are. That is
the crux of the problem. Many people have
been educated out of knowing what their feelings are. When they hated, they were told it
was only dislike. When they were afraid, they
were told there was nothing to be afraid of.
When they felt pain, they were advised to be
brave and smile. Many of our popular songs tell
us "Pretend you are happy when you are not."

What is suggested in the place of this pre-
tense? Truth. Emotional education can help
children to *know what they feel*. It is more
important for a child to know what he feels
than why he feels it. When he knows clearly
what his feelings are, he is less likely to feel "all
mixed-up" inside.

Conversing with children

PROVIDING A MIRROR TO THE PERSONALITY

How can we help a child to know his feelings? We can do so by serving as a mirror to his emotions. A child learns about his physical likeness by seeing his image in a mirror. He learns about his emotional likeness by hearing his feelings reflected by us.

The function of a mirror is to reflect an image as it is, without adding flattery or faults. We do not want a mirror to tell us, "You look terrible. Your eyes are bloodshot and your face is puffy. Altogether you are a mess. You'd better do something about yourself." After a few exposures to such a magic mirror, we would avoid it like the plague. From a mirror we want an image, not a sermon. We may not like the image we see; still, we would rather decide for ourselves our next cosmetic move.

The function of an emotional mirror is to reflect feelings as they are, without distortion:

"It looks as though you are very angry."

"It sounds like you hate him very much."

"It seems that you are disgusted with the whole set-up."

To a child who has such feelings, these statements are most helpful. They show him clearly what his feelings are. Clarity of image, whether in a looking glass or in an emotional mirror, provides opportunity for self-initiated grooming and change.

40

New ways of praise and criticism

THE CASE OF THE FLYING ASHTRAY:
A STORY WITH A MORAL

It was early in the morning, the Monday after Thanksgiving weekend. The woman on the telephone sounded frantic. "Figure this out," she said, "if you can. Here we are in the car, the whole family. We drove four hundred miles from Pittsburgh to New York. In the back of the car, Ivan behaved like an angel, quiet and deep in thought. I said to myself, 'He deserves some praise.' We were just entering the Lincoln Tunnel when I turned to him and said, 'You are such a good boy, Ivan. You behaved so well. I am proud of you.'

"A minute later the sky fell on us. Ivan pulled out an ashtray and spilled its contents all over us. The ashes, the cigarette butts, and the smoke kept coming, like atomic fallout. We were in the tunnel, in heavy traffic, and we were choking. I could have killed him. If it were not for the other cars around us, I would have murdered him on the spot. And what burned me up most was that I had just praised him so sincerely. Isn't praise good for children any more?"

Weeks later Ivan himself revealed the cause of the explosion. All the way home he had been wondering how he could get rid of his younger brother, who was snuggled up between mother and father in the front of the car. Finally the idea occurred to him that if their car were jackknifed in the middle, he and his parents would be safe, but the baby would be cut in two. Just then mother had congratulated him on his goodness. The praise made him feel guilty, and he wanted desperately to show that he did not deserve it. He looked around, saw the ashtray, and the rest had followed instantly.

PRAISING ACCOMPLISHMENTS OR PERSONALITY?

Most people believe that praise builds up a child's confidence and makes him feel secure. In actuality, praise may result in tension and misbehavior. Why? Many children have, from time to time, destructive wishes about members of their family. When parents tell a child, "You are such a good boy," he may not be able to accept it because his own picture of himself is quite different. In his own eyes, he cannot be "good" when only recently he wished that his mother had a zipper on her mouth or that his brother would spend next weekend in the hospital. In fact, the more he is praised, the more he misbehaves in order to show his "true self." Parents frequently report that just after praising a child for good deportment, he starts to act wild, as though to disprove their compliment. It is possible that "acting-up" is the child's way of communicating his private reservations about his public image.

Desirable and undesirable praise.—Does this mean that praise is now "out"? Not at all. It does mean, however, that praise, like penicillin, must not be administered haphazardly. There are rules and cautions that govern the handling of potent medicines—rules about timing and dosage, cautions about possible allergic reactions. There are similar regulations about the administration of emotional medicine. The single most important rule is that praise deal only with the child's efforts and accomplishments, *not* with his character and personality.

When a boy cleans up the yard, it is only natural to comment on how hard he has worked, and on how good the yard looks. It is highly unrelated, and inappropriate, to tell him how good he is. Words of praise should mirror for the child a *realistic* picture of his *accomplishments*, not a Madison Avenue image of his personality.

New ways of praise and criticism

The following example illustrates desirable praise: Jim, age eight, did a good job cleaning up the yard. He raked the leaves, removed the garbage, and rearranged the tools. Mother was impressed and expressed her appreciation of his efforts and achievements:

MOTHER: The yard was so dirty. I didn't believe it could be cleaned up in one day.

JIM: I did it!

MOTHER: It was full of leaves and garbage and things.

JIM: I cleaned it all up.

MOTHER: What a job!

JIM: Yeah, it sure was.

MOTHER: The yard is so clean now, it is a pleasure to look at it.

JIM: It's nice.

MOTHER: Thank you, son.

JIM (*with a mile-wide smile*): You are welcome.

Mother's words made Jim feel glad of his efforts and proud of his accomplishments. That evening he could not wait for his father to come home in order to show him the cleaned-up yard and again to feel within himself the pride of a task well done.

In contrast, the following words of praise addressed to the child's personality are unhelpful:

"You are such a wonderful child."

"You are truly mother's little helper."

"What would mother do without you?"

Such comments may threaten a child and

cause him anxiety.* He may feel that he is far from being wonderful and that he is unable to live up to this label. So, instead of fearfully waiting to be exposed as a fraud, he may decide to lessen his burden immediately by a confession of misbehavior.

Direct praise of personality, like direct sunlight, is uncomfortable and blinding. It is embarrassing for a person to be told that he is wonderful, angelic, generous, and humble. He feels called upon to deny at least part of the praise. Publicly, he cannot stand up and say, "Thank you, I accept your words that I am wonderful." Privately, too, he must reject such praise. He cannot honestly say to himself, "I am wonderful. I am good and strong and generous and humble."

He may not only reject the praise but may have some second thoughts about those who have praised him: "If they find me so great, they cannot be so smart."

OUR WORDS AND THE CHILD'S INFERENCES

Praise should deal, not with the child's personality attributes, but with his efforts and

* Praise may also be threatening to adults. In "Robert Frost Confronts Khrushchev," F. D. Reeve states: "The honors Frost received made him nervous, for honors . . . may be terrifying: it may mean you have to do something better next time, something which you fear will fail." *Atlantic Monthly* (September, 1963), p. 38.

achievements. Our comments should be so phrased that the child draws from them positive inferences about his personality. Kenny, age ten, helped his father fix up the basement. In the process he had to move heavy furniture.

FATHER: The workbench is so heavy. It is hard to move.

KENNY (*with pride*): But I did it.

FATHER: It takes a lot of strength.

KENNY (*flexing his muscles*): I am strong.

In this example, father commented on the difficulty of the task. It was the child himself who drew the inference about his personal power. Had his father said, "You are so strong, son," Kenny might have replied, "No, I am not. There are stronger boys than I in my class." A fruitless, if not bitter, argument might have followed.

SILENT STATEMENTS AND SELF-IMAGE

Praise has two parts: our words and the child's inferences. Our words should state clearly that we appreciate the child's effort, work, achievement, help, consideration, or creation. Our words should be so framed that the child will almost inevitably draw from them a realistic conclusion about his personality. Our words should be like a magic canvas upon which a child cannot help but paint a positive

48

picture of himself. The following examples illustrate this point:

Helpful praise: Thank you for washing the car, it looks new again.
Possible inference: I did a good job. My work is appreciated.
(Unhelpful praise: You are an angel.)

Helpful praise: I liked your get-well card. It was so pretty and witty.
Possible inference: I have good taste, I can rely on my choices.
(Unhelpful praise: You are *always* so considerate.)

Helpful praise: Your poem spoke to my heart.
Possible inference: I am glad I can write poems.
(Unhelpful praise: You are a good poet for your age.)

Helpful praise: The bookcase that you built looks beautiful.
Possible inference: I am capable.
(Unhelpful praise: You are such a good carpenter.)

Helpful praise: Your letter brought me a great joy.
Possible inference: I can bring happiness to others.

49

(Unhelpful praise: When it comes to letters, you are wonderful.)

Helpful praise: I appreciate greatly your washing the dishes today.
Possible inference: I am helpful.
(Unhelpful praise: You did a better job than the maid.)

Helpful praise: Thanks for telling me that I overpaid you. I appreciate it very much.
Possible inference: I'm glad I was honest.
(Unhelpful praise: You are such an honest child.)

Helpful praise: Your composition gave me several new ideas.
Possible inference: I can be original.
(Unhelpful praise: You write well for your grade. Of course, you still have a lot to learn.

Such descriptive statements and the child's positive conclusions are the building blocks of mental health. What he concludes about himself in response to our words, the child later restates silently to himself. Realistic positive statements repeated inwardly by the child determine to a large extent his good opinion of himself and the world around him.

CRITICISM: CONSTRUCTIVE AND DESTRUCTIVE

When is criticism constructive and when is it destructive? Constructive criticism confines itself to pointing out how to do what has to be done, entirely omitting negative remarks about the personality of the child.

Larry, age ten, inadvertently spilled a glass of milk on the breakfast table.

MOTHER: You are old enough to know how to hold a glass! How many times have I told you to be careful!

FATHER: He can't help it—he is clumsy. He always was and he always will be.

Larry spilled five cents' worth of milk, but the caustic ridicule that followed the accident may cost much more in terms of loss of confidence. When things go wrong is not the right time to teach an offender about his personality. When things go wrong, it is best to deal only with the event, not with the person.

How to behave when a child misbehaves.— When Martin, age eight, accidentally spilled his milk on the table, his mother commented calmly, "I see the milk is spilled. Here is another glass of milk, and here is a sponge." Mother got up and handed the milk and the sponge to her son. Martin looked up at her in relief and disbelief. He muttered, "Gee, thanks, Mom." He cleaned up the table while mother helped him.

She did not add cutting comments or useless admonitions. Mother related, "I was tempted to say, 'Next time be careful,' but when I saw how grateful he was for my benevolent silence, I said nothing. In the past, the cry over spilled milk would have spoiled the mood for the entire day."

HOW THINGS GO WRONG

In many homes, storms between parents and children develop in a regular and predictable sequence. The child does or says something "wrong." The parent reacts with something insulting. The child replies with something worse. The parent retorts with high-pitched threats or with high-handed punishment. And the free-for-all is on.

Nathaniel, age nine, was playing with an empty teacup.

MOTHER: You'll break it. You are always breaking things.

NATHANIEL: No, I won't.

Just then the cup fell on the floor and broke.

MOTHER: For crying out loud, you are so stupid. You break everything in the house.

NATHANIEL: You are stupid, too. You broke father's electric razor.

MOTHER: You called mother stupid! You are so rude.

52

NATHANIEL: You are rude. You called me stupid first.

MOTHER: Not another word from you! Go up to your room immediately!

NATHANIEL: Go ahead, make me!

At this direct challenge to her authority, mother became enraged. She grabbed her son and started spanking him in fury. While attempting to escape, Nathaniel pushed his mother into a glass door. The glass broke and cut mother's hand. The sight of blood threw Nathaniel into a panic. He ran out of the house and was not found until late in the evening. Needless to say, the whole household was upset. No one in the house slept well that night.

Whether or not Nathaniel learned to avoid empty teacups was less important than the negative lesson that he learned about himself and his mother. The question is: Was this battle necessary? Was the fighting inevitable? Or is it possible to handle such incidents more wisely?

Upon seeing her son rolling the cup, mother could have removed it and directed him to a more suitable substitute, such as a ball. Or when the cup broke, she could have helped her son dispose of the pieces, with comments to the effect that cups break easily and who would have thought that such a small cup could make such a big mess. The surprise of such a low-toned sentence might have sent Nathaniel into atonement and apology for the mishap. In the absence of screams and spankings, he may even

53

have had the presence of mind to conclude for himself that cups are not for rolling.

Minor mishaps and major values.—From minor mishaps children can learn major lessons in values. A child needs to learn from his parents to distinguish between events that are merely unpleasant and annoying and those that are tragic or catastrophic. Many parents react to a broken egg as to a broken leg, to a shattered window as to a shattered heart. Minor misfortunes should be pointed out as such to children:

"So you lost your glove again. That is annoying, because gloves cost money. It's regrettable, but it is not a catastrophe."

A lost glove need not lead to a lost temper, a torn shirt need not serve as a prop for a do-it-yourself Greek tragedy.

ABUSIVE ADJECTIVES: WHAT'S IN A NAME?

Abusive adjectives, like poisonous arrows, are to be used only against enemies, not against little children. When a person says. "This is an ugly chair," nothing happens to the chair. It is neither insulted nor embarrassed. It stays just as it is regardless of the adjective attached to it. However, when a child is called ugly or stupid or clumsy, something does happen to the child. There are reactions in his body and in his soul. There are resentment and anger and hate.

There are fantasies of revenge. There is guilt about the fantasies, and anxiety stemming from the guilt. And there may be undesirable behavior and symptoms. (See Chapter 7, page 150) In short, there is a chain of reactions that makes the child and his parents miserable.

When a child is called clumsy, he may at first retort with, "No, I am not clumsy." But, more often than not, he believes his parents, and he comes to think of himself as a clumsy person. When he happens to stumble or to fall, he may say aloud to himself, "You are so clumsy." He may, from then on, avoid situations in which agility is required because he is convinced that he is too clumsy to succeed.

When a child is repeatedly told by his parents or teachers that he is stupid, he comes to believe it. He starts thinking of himself as such. He then gives up intellectual efforts, feeling that his escape from ridicule lies in avoiding contest and competition. His safety hinges on not trying. His motto in life becomes: "If I don't try, I can't fail."

HANDLING OUR OWN ANGER

In our own childhood, we were not taught how to deal with anger as a fact of life. We were made to feel guilty for experiencing anger and sinful for expressing it. We were led to believe that to be angry is to be bad. Anger was not merely a misdemeanor: it was a felony.

With our own children, we try to be patient; in fact, so patient that sooner or later we must explode. We are afraid that our anger may be harmful to children, so we hold it in, as a skin diver holds his breath. In both instances, however, the capacity for holding in is rather limited.

Anger, like the common cold, is a recurrent problem. We may not like it, but we cannot ignore it. We may know it intimately, but we cannot prevent its appearance. Anger arises in predictable sequences and situations, yet it always seems sudden and unexpected. And, though it may not last long, anger seems eternal for the moment.

When we lose our temper, we act as though we have lost our sanity. We say and do things to our children that we would hesitate to inflict on an enemy. We yell, insult, and hit below the belt. When the fanfare is over, we feel guilty and we solemnly resolve never to render a repeat performance. But anger soon strikes again, undoing our good intentions. Once more we lash out at those to whose welfare we have dedicated our life and fortune.

Resolutions about not becoming angry are worse than futile. They only add fuel to fire. Anger, like a hurricane, is a fact of life to be acknowledged and prepared for. The peaceful home, like the hoped-for warless world, does not depend on a sudden benevolent change in human nature. It does depend on deliberate procedures that methodically reduce tensions before they lead to explosions.

There is a place for parental anger in child education. In fact, failure to get angry at certain moments would only convey to the child indifference, not goodness. Those who care cannot altogether shun anger. This does not mean that children can withstand floods of fury and violence; it only means that they can stand and understand anger which says: "There are limits to my tolerance."

For parents, anger is a costly emotion: to be worth its price it should not be employed without profit. Anger should not be used so that it increases with expression. The medication must not be worse than the disease. Anger should so come out that it brings some relief to the parent, some insight to the child, and no harmful side effects to either of them. Thus we should not bawl out a child in front of his friends; it only makes him act up more, which in turn makes us angrier. We are not interested in creating or perpetuating waves of anger, defiance, retaliation, and revenge. On the contrary, we want to get our point across and let the stormy clouds evaporate.

Three steps to survival.—To prepare ourselves in times of peace to deal with times of stress, we should acknowledge the following truths:

1. We accept the fact that children will make us angry.

2. We are entitled to our anger without guilt or shame.

3. Except for one safeguard, we are entitled to express what we feel. We can express our angry feelings *provided* we do not attack the child's personality or character.

These assumptions should be implemented in concrete procedures for dealing with anger. The first step in handling turbulent feelings is to identify them loudly by name. This gives a warning to whomever it may concern to make amends or to take precautions.

"I feel annoyed."

"I feel irritated."

If our short statements and long faces have not brought relief, we proceed to the second step. We express our anger with increasing intensity:

"I feel angry."

"I feel very angry."

"I feel very, very angry."

"I feel furious."

Sometimes the mere statement of our feelings (without explanations) stops the child from acting up. At other times it may be necessary to proceed to the third step, which is to give the reason for our anger, to state our inner reactions, and *wishful* actions.

"When I see the shoes and the socks and the shirts and the sweaters spread all over the floor, I get angry, I get furious. I feel like opening the window and throwing the whole mess into the middle of the street."

"It makes me angry to see you hit your brother. I get so mad inside myself that I see red. I start boiling. I can never allow you to hurt him."

"When I see all of you rush away from dinner to watch TV, and leave me with the dirty dishes and greasy pans, I feel murderous! I get so mad I fume inside! I feel like taking every dish and breaking it on the TV set!"

"When I call you for dinner and you don't come, I get angry. I get very angry. I say to myself, 'I cooked a good meal and I want some appreciation, not frustration!' "

This approach allows parents to give vent to their anger without causing damage. On the contrary, it may even illustrate an important lesson in how to express anger safely. The child may learn that his own anger is not catastrophic, that it can be discharged without destroying anyone. This lesson will require more than just expression of anger by parents. It will require that parents point out to their children acceptable channels of emotional expression and demonstrate to them safe and respectable ways of liquidating anger. The problem of finding suitable substitutes for destructive feelings will be dealt with at length in Chapter 5.

CHAPTER 3

Avoiding self-defeating patterns

Certain patterns of relating to children are almost always self-defeating; not only do they fail to attain our long-term goals, but they often create havoc at home here and now. The self-defeating patterns include threats, bribes, promises, sarcasm, sermons on lying and stealing, and rude teaching of politeness.

THREATS

Invitations to misbehavior.—To children threats are invitations to repeat a forbidden act. When a child is told, "If you do it once more . . ." he does not hear the words "if you." He hears only "do it once more." Sometimes he interprets it as "Mother expects me to do it once more, or she'll be disappointed."

63

Such warnings—fair as they may seem to adults—are worse than useless. They make sure that an obnoxious act will be repeated. A warning serves as a challenge to the child's autonomy. If he has any self-respect he must transgress again, to show to himself and to others that he is not a sissy.

Oliver, age five, kept on throwing a ball at the window in spite of many warnings. Finally mother said, "If the ball hits the window once more, I'll beat the living daylights out of you. I promise." A minute later, the crash of breaking glass told mother that her warning had had an effect: the ball had hit the glass for the last time. The scene that followed this sequence of threats, promises, and misbehavior can easily be imagined. In contrast, the following incident is an illustration of effective handling of misbehavior without resort to threats.

Peter, age seven, shot the popgun at his baby brother. Mother said, "Not at the baby. Shoot at the target." Peter shot at the baby again. Mother took the gun away. To Peter she said, "People are not for shooting."

Mother did what she felt had to be done to protect the baby and at the same time uphold her standards of acceptable behavior. Peter learned the consequences of his actions without any damage to his ego. The implied alternatives were obvious: to shoot at the target or to lose the privilege of having the gun.

In this incident, mother avoided the usual pitfalls. She did not embark on the predictable trail to failure: "Stop it. Peter! Don't you know better than to shoot at your brother? Don't you have a better target? If you do it once more, you hear, once more, you'll never see the gun again!" Unless the child is very meek, his response to such an admonition will be a repetition of the forbidden. The scene that would then follow need not be described—it can easily be reconstructed by every parent.

BRIBES

The "if-then" fallacy.—Similarly self-defeating is the approach that explicitly tells a child that *if* he will (or will not) do something, *then* he will get a reward:

"*If* you are nice to baby brother, *then* I'll take you to the movies."

"*If* you stop wetting your bed, *then* I'll get you a bicycle for Christmas."

"*If* you learn the poem, *then* I'll take you sailing."

This "if-then" approach may occasionally spur the child toward an immediate goal. But it seldom, if ever, inspires him toward continual efforts. Our very words convey to him that we doubt his ability to change for the better. "If you learn the poem" means "We are not sure you can." "If you stop wetting" means "We don't think you can do it."

There are also some moral objections to re-

wards that are used to bribe. Dorothy Baruch*
tells of a boy who said, "I get what I want by
keeping mother thinking I'll be bad. Of course,
I have to be bad often enough to convince her
she is not paying me for nothing."

Such reasoning may soon lead to bargaining
and blackmail, and to ever increasing demands
for prizes and fringe benefits in exchange for
"good" behavior. Some parents have been so
conditioned by their children that they do not
dare come home from a shopping trip without a
present. They are greeted by the children, not
with a "hello," but with a "what-did-you-bring-
me?"

Rewards are most helpful and more enjoy-
able when they are unannounced in advance,
when they come as a surprise, when they represent recognition and appreciation.

PROMISES

Unrealistic expectations and practices.—
Promises should neither be made to, nor de-
manded of, children. Why such a taboo on
promises? Relations with our children should
be built on trust. When a parent must make
promises to emphasize that he means what he
says, then he is as much as admitting that his
"unpromised" word is not trustworthy. Prom-

* See bibliography.

ises build up unrealistic expectations in children.When a child is promised a visit to the zoo, he considers it a commitment that the day will not be rainy, that the car will not be out of order, and that he will not be sick. Since life is not without mishaps, children come to feel betrayed and convinced that parents cannot be trusted. The relentless complaint "but you promised!" is painfully familiar to parents who belatedly wish they had not.

Promises about the future good behavior or the cessation of past misbehavior should not be requested or extracted from children. When a child makes a promise that is not his own, he draws a check on a bank in which he has no account. We should not encourage such fraudulent practices.

SARCASM

A sound barrier to learning.—A serious mental health hazard is a parent with a gift for sarcasm. A wizard with words, he erects his own sound barrier to effective communication:

"How many times must I repeat the same thing? Are you deaf? Then why don't you listen?"

"You are so rude. Were you brought up in a jungle? That's where you belong, you know."

"What's the matter with you anyhow? Are

you crazy or just stupid? I know where you'll end up!"

Such a parent may not even be aware that his remarks are attacks that invite counterattacks, that his comments block communication by stirring children to preoccupation with revenge fantasies.

Bitter sarcasm and cutting clichés have no place in child upbringing. It is best to avoid statements such as, "You have grown too big for your breeches"; "You have a swelled head"; "Who do you think you are anyway?" Wittingly or unwittingly, we should not deflate the child's status in his own eyes and in the eyes of his peers.

A POLICY ON LYING

Parents are enraged when children lie, especially when the lie is obvious and the liar is clumsy. It is infuriating to hear a child insist that he did not touch the paint or eat the chocolate when the evidence is all over his shirt and face.

Why do children lie?—Sometimes they lie because they are not allowed to tell the truth. When a child tells his mother that he hates his brother, she may spank him for telling the truth. If he turns around then and there and declares the obvious lie that he now loves his brother, mother may reward him with a hug and a kiss. What is the child to conclude from such an experience? He may conclude that truth hurts, that dishonesty rewards, and that mother loves little liars.

If we want to teach honesty, then we must be prepared to listen to bitter truths as well as to pleasant truths. If a child is to grow up honest, he must not be encouraged to lie about his feelings, be they positive, negative, or ambivalent. It is from our reactions to his expressed feelings that the child learns whether or not honesty is the best policy.

Lies that tell truths.—When punished for truth, children lie in self-defense. They also lie to give themselves in fantasy what they lack in reality. Lies tell truths about fears and hopes. They reveal what one would like to be or to do. To a discerning ear, lies reveal what they intend to conceal. A mature reaction to a lie should reflect understanding of its meaning, rather than denial of its content or condemnation of its author. The information gained from the lie can be used to help the child to distinguish between reality and wishful thinking.

When a little boy informs us that he received a live elephant for Christmas, it is more helpful to reply, "You *wish* you did," than to prove that he is a liar.

"You *wish* you had an elephant!"

"You *wish* you had your own zoo!"

"You *wish* you had a jungle full of animals!"

"And what did you get for Christmas?"

Provoked lies.—Parents should not ask questions that are likely to cause defensive lying. Children resent being interrogated by a parent, especially when they suspect that the answers are already known. They hate questions that are traps, questions that force them to choose between an awkward lie or an embarrassing confession.

Quentin, age seven, broke a new gun given to him by his father. He became frightened and hid the broken pieces in the basement. When father found the remains of the gun, he fired off a few questions that led to an explosion.

FATHER: Where is your new gun?

QUENTIN: It's somewhere.

FATHER: I didn't see you playing with it.

QUENTIN: I don't know where it is.

FATHER: Find it. I want to see it.

QUENTIN: Maybe someone stole the gun.

FATHER: You are a damned liar! You broke the gun! Don't think you can get away with it. If there's one thing I hate, it's a liar!

And father gave him a spanking he would long remember.

This was an unnecessary battle. Instead of sneakingly playing detective and prosecutor, father would have been more helpful to his son by saying:

"I see your new gun is broken."

"It did not last long."

"It's a pity. It's expensive."

The child might have learned some valuable lessons: "Father understands. I can tell him my troubles. I must take better care of his gifts."

DEALING WITH DISHONESTY

Our policy towards lying is clear: on the one hand, we should not play D.A. or ask for confessions or make a federal case out of a tall story. On the other hand, we should not hesitate to call a spade a spade. When we find that the child's library book is overdue, we should not ask, "Have you returned the book to the library? Are you sure? How come it's still on your desk?"

Instead, we state, "I see your library book is overdue."

When the school informs us that our child has failed his arithmetic test, we should not ask him. "Did you pass your arithmetic exam? Are you sure? Well, lying won't help you this time! We talked with your teacher and we know that you failed miserably."

Instead, we tell our child directly, "The arithmetic teacher told us that you have failed the test. We are worried and wonder how to be of help."

In short, we do not provoke the child into defensive lying, nor do we intentionally set up opportunities for lying. When a child does lie, our reaction should be not hysterical and moralistic, but factual and realistic. We want our child to learn that there is no need to lie to us.

71

STEALING

It is not uncommon for young children to bring home things that do not belong to them. When the "theft" is discovered, it is important to avoid sermons and dramatics. The young child can be guided into the path of righteousness with dignity. He is told calmly and firmly:

"The truck belongs to someone else, give it back to him."

"The gun does not belong to you. Take it back."

When a child "steals" candy and puts it in his pocket, it is best to confront him unemotionally: "The lollypop in your left pocket has to stay in the store." If the child denies having the candy, we point and repeat the statement: "The lollypop in this pocket belongs to the store. Put it on the shelf." If he refuses, we take it out of his pocket, saying, "It belongs to the store. It has to stay here."

The wrong question and the right statement— When you are *sure* that your child stole money from your pocketbook, it is best not to ask him, but to tell him, about it: "You took a dollar from my pocketbook. Give it back." When the money is retrieved, he is told sternly, "When you need money, ask me, and we will talk it over." If the child denies the act, we do not argue with him or beg him for a confession; we

72

tell him: "You took the money, return it." If the money has already been spent, the discussion should focus on ways of reimbursement, in chores or by reduction in allowance.

It is important to avoid calling the child a thief and a liar or prophesying that he will end up in Sing Sing. It is not helpful to ask the child, "Why did you do it?" He, himself, may not know his motivation, and pressure to tell "why" can only result in another lie.

It is more helpful to point out that you expect him to discuss with you his need for money:

"I am disappointed that you did not tell me that you needed a dollar."

"When you need money, come and tell me. We'll talk it over."

If your child has eaten cookies from the forbidden jar, and there is a mustache of sugar on his face, do not ask him questions such as:

"Did anybody take cookies from the jar?"

"Did you by any chance see who took them? Did you eat one? Are you sure?"

Such questions usually push the child into making up lies, which adds insult to our injury. The rule is that *when we know the answer, we do not ask the question.* It is better to state openly:

"Son, you ate the cookies. I told you not to. I am angry and I am disappointed."

The last statement constitutes adequate and desirable punishment. It leaves the child with discomfort, and the responsibility to do something about his misbehavior.

TEACHING POLITENESS: RUDELY OR POLITELY?

Private models and public manners.—
Politeness is both a character trait and a social skill; it is acquired through identification with, and imitation of, parents who are themselves polite. Under all conditions, politeness must be taught politely. Yet parents frequently teach it rudely. When a child forgets to say "thank you," parents point it out to him in front of other people, which is impolite, to say the least. Parents hasten to remind their child to say "good-bye" even before they themselves bid farewell.

Six-year-old Robert has just been handed a wrapped gift. Full of curiosity, he squeezes the box to find out what is in it.

MOTHER: Robert, stop it! You are spoiling the gift! What do you say when you get a present?

ROBERT: (*angrily*): Thank you!

MOTHER: That's a good boy.

Mother could have taught this bit of politeness less rudely and more effectively. She could have said, "Thank you, Aunt Patricia, for this lovely gift." It is conceivable that Robert might have followed with his own thank you. If he had failed to do so, mother could have dealt

74

with social amenities later when they were by themselves. She could have said, "It was considerate of Aunt Patricia to think of you and get you a gift. Let us write her a thank-you note. She will be glad that we thought of her."

While more complicated than a direct reprimand, this approach is more efficient. The niceties of the art of living cannot be conveyed with a sledgehammer.

When children interrupt adult conversation, adults usually react angrily: "Don't be rude! It is impolite to interrupt!" However, interrupting the interrupter is also impolite. Parents should not be rude in the process of enforcing child politeness. Perhaps it would be better to state, "I would like to finish telling my story. Then you will have your turn."

No good purpose is served by telling a child that he is rude. Contrary to hope, it does not steer him into politeness. The danger is that he will accept our evaluation and make it a part of his self-image. Once he thinks of himself as a rude boy, he will continue to live up to this image. It is only natural for rude boys to behave rudely.

Visits to homes of friends or relatives provide opportunities for demonstrating politeness to children. Visiting should be fun for the parent and the child. This can best be achieved when the burden of responsibility for the child's *behavior* is left to the child and the host. (Our help will be confined to voicing understanding of the child's wishes and feelings.)

75

Avoiding self-defeating patterns

Children learn that we are loath to reprimand them in the homes of others. Trusting geography, they choose these locations to act up. This strategy can be counteracted best by letting the host set the rules of his own house and carry out their enforcement. When a child jumps on the sofa in Aunt Mary's house, let Aunt Mary decide whether or not the sofa is for jumping, and let her invoke the limit. A child is more likely to obey when restrictions are invoked by outsiders. Mother, relieved of disciplinary obligation, can help the child by restating the limit privately: "These are the rules here."

This policy can be implemented only when there is agreement between host and guest as to their respective areas of responsibility. It is the right, and the responsibility, of the host to demand compliance with the rules of his home. It is the responsibility of the visiting mother to relinquish temporarily her role of disciplinarian. By appropriate nonintervention, mother helps the child perceive the reality of the situation.

✿ CHAPTER 4

Responsibility and independence

RESPONSIBILITY: CHORES AND VALUES

Parents everywhere are looking for ways of teaching responsibility to children. In many homes, daily chores are expected to provide the solution to this problem. Emptying trash baskets and mowing lawns are believed to be especially effective in making boys responsible; dishwashing and bedmaking are alleged to lay a foundation of responsibility in girls. In actuality, such chores, though important for home management, may have no positive effect on creating a sense of responsibility. On the contrary, in some homes the daily tasks result in daily battles that bring anguish and anger to both children and parents. Forceful insistence on the performance of chores may result in obedience and in cleaner kitchens and yards, but it may have an undesirable influence on the molding of character.

The plain fact is that responsibility cannot be imposed. It can only grow from within, fed and directed by values absorbed at home and in the community. Responsibility that is not anchored in positive values can be antisocial and destructive. Hoodlums often show great loyalty and high responsibility in relation to one another and to their gang. Members of the Mafia, for instance, take their duties in dead earnest; they carry out commands, give legal aid to needy associates, and take care of prisoners' families.

The wellspring of responsibility.—While we wish our children to be responsible persons, we want their responsibility to spring from ultimate values, among which are reverence for life and concern for human welfare. In more familiar words, responsibility must be based on respect for life, liberty, and the pursuit of happiness. We do not usually consider the problem of responsibility in its larger framework. We see responsibility, or the lack of it, in much more concrete terms: in our child's messy room, tardy school attendance, sloppy homework, reluctant piano practice, sulky disobediance, or bad manners.

Yet a child may be polite, keep himself and his room clean, do his assignments with precision, and still make irresponsible decisions. This is especially true of children who are always told what to do and who therefore have little opportunity to exercise judgment, to make choices, and to develop inner standards.

The child's inner emotional reaction to our

instruction is a decisive element in how much he learns of what we want him to know. Values cannot be taught directly. They are absorbed, and become part of the child, only through his identification with, and emulation of, persons who gain his love and respect.

Thus, the problem of responsibility in children is referred back to the parent, or more precisely to the parent's values as expressed in his child-rearing practices. The question to consider now is: Are there any definite attitudes and practices that are likely to create a desired sense of responsibility in our children? The rest of the chapter is an attempt to answer this question from a psychological point of view.

DESIRABLE GOALS AND DAILY PRACTICES

Responsibility in children starts with the parent's attitude and skills. The attitudes include a willingness to allow children to feel *all* their feelings; the skills include an ability to demonstrate to children acceptable ways of coping with feelings.

The difficulties entailed in meeting these two requirements are most formidable. Our own parents and teachers have not adequately prepared us for dealing with emotions. They themselves did not know how to cope with strong feelings. When confronted with turbulent emotions in children, they tried to deny,

81

disown, suppress, or prettify them. They used pat phrases that were not too helpful:

Denial: You don't really mean what you say; you know you love your little brother.

Disowning: It's not you, it's the devil in you that is acting up.

Suppression: If you mention the word "hate" once more, you'll get the spanking of your life. A nice child does not feel like that.

Prettifying: You don't really hate your brother. Maybe you dislike him. You should rise above such feelings.

Such statements ignore the fact that emotions, like rivers, cannot be stopped, only diverted. Strong feelings, like the rising waters of the Mississippi, cannot be denied, reasoned with, or talked out of, existence. To attempt to ignore them is to invite disaster. They must be recognized and their power acknowledged. They must be treated with respect and diverted with ingenuity. Thus channeled, they may electrify our existence and bring light and joy into our lives.

These are lofty goals. The question still remains: What steps can we take to bridge the gulf between desirable goals and daily practices? Where do we start?

LONG-TERM AND SHORT-TERM PROGRAMS

The answer seems to lie in making a program that is a combination of long-term and short-term efforts. Immediately, we need clear recognition that character education depends on our *relationship* with our children and that character traits cannot be transmitted by words but must be demonstrated.

The first step in the long-term program is a determination to become interested in what children are thinking and feeling inwardly, and not just in their outward compliance or rebellion.

How can we become aware of what children think and feel inside?

Children give us clues. Their feelings come through in word and in tone, in gesture and in posture. All we need is an ear to listen, an eye to behold, a heart to feel.

Our inner motto is: Let me understand. Let me show that I understand. Let me show in words that do not automatically criticize or condemn.

When a child comes home from school silent, slow, and dragging, we can tell by his steps that something unpleasant happened to him. Following our motto, we shall *not* start our conversation with a critical comment, such as:

"What's the sour puss for?"

"What kind of face is that?"

"What did you do, lose your best friend?"

"What did you do this time?"

"What trouble are you in today?"

Since we are interested in the child's inner reaction, we shall avoid comments that only create resentment and hate inside him, comments that make him wish that the whole world would drop dead.

Instead, the parent can show understanding by saying any of the following:

"Something unpleasant happened to you."

"It was not a good day for you."

"It was a hard day."

"Someone gave you a hard time."

These statements are preferable to such questions as, "What's the matter with you? What happened?" The questions convey curiosity, the statements convey sympathy.

There is no escape from the fact that a child learns what he lives. If he lives with criticism, he does not learn responsibility. He learns to condemn himself and to find fault with others. He learns to doubt his own judgment, to disparage his own ability, and to distrust the intentions of others. And above all, he learns to live with continual expectation of impending doom.

FROM WAR TO PEACE

Parents who are in the midst of a declared or undeclared war with their children over chores and responsibilities should recognize the fact that this war cannot be won. Children have more time and energy to resist us than we have to coerce them. Even if we win a battle and succeed in enforcing our will, they may retaliate by becoming spiritless and neurotic, or rebellious and delinquent.

There is only one way in which we can win: by winning the children over. This task may seem impossible: it is merely difficult, and we have the capacity to accomplish it. Even if we do not presently have friendly relations with a child, such relations can be built in the near future.

Parents can initiate favorable changes in their child by:

1. *Listening with sensitivity*. Children experience frustration and resentment when parents seem uninterested in their feelings and thoughts. As a result, they conclude that their own ideas are stupid and unworthy of attention and that they themselves are neither lovable nor loved.

A parent who listens with attentiveness conveys to his child that his ideas are valued and that he is respected. Such respect gives the child a sense of self-worth. The feeling of personal worth enables the child to deal more effectively with the world of events and people.

2. *Preventing "grapes of wrath."* Parents should consciously avoid words and comments that create hate and resentment.

Insults: You are a disgrace to your school and no credit to your family.

Name Calling: Bum, big shot, shrimp, idiot.

Prophesying: You will end up in a federal penitentiary, that's where you'll end up.

85

Threats: If you don't settle down you can forget about your allowance.

Accusations: You are *always* the first to start trouble.

Bossing: Shut up, and let me tell you a thing or two.

3. *Stating feelings and thoughts without attacking.* In troublesome situations, parents are more effective when they state their own feelings and thoughts without attacking their child's personality and dignity. (See Chapter 2, page 54.)

When parents listen with sensitivity, suspend cutting comments, and state their feelings and requirements without insult, a process of change is initiated in the child. The sympathetic atmosphere draws the child nearer to the parents; their attitudes and fairness, consideration, and civility are noticed and emulated. These changes will not occur overnight, but the efforts will ultimately be rewarded.

In adopting these new attitudes and practices, a parent will accomplish a large part of educating his child for responsibility. And yet, example alone is not enough. A sense of responsibility is attained by each child through his own efforts and experience. While the parent's example creates the favorable attitude and climate for learning, specific experiences consolidate the learning to make it part of the child's character. Therefore, it is important to determine what specific responsibilities to give to children at different levels of maturity.

RESPONSIBILITY: VOICE AND CHOICE

Children are not born with a built-in sense of responsibility. Neither do they acquire it automatically at a certain prescribed age. Responsibility, like piano playing, is attained slowly and over many long years. It requires daily practice in exercising judgment and in making choices about matters appropriate to one's age and comprehension.

Conflict areas and realms of responsibility.— Education for responsibility can start very early in the child's life. Responsibility is fostered by allowing children a voice, and wherever indicated, a choice, in matters that affect them. A deliberate distinction is made here between a voice and a choice. There are matters that fall entirely within the child's realm of responsibility. In such matters he should have his choice. There are matters affecting the child's welfare that are exclusively within our realm of responsibility. In such matters he may have a voice, but not a choice. We make the choice for him— while helping him to accept the inevitable.

What is needed now is a clear distinction between these two realms of responsibility. Let us examine several areas in which conflicts between parents and children are not uncommon.

FOOD

Even a two-year-old can be asked whether he wants half a glass of milk or a full glass of milk. A four-year-old can be given a choice between half an apple or a whole apple. And a six-year-old can decide for himself whether he wants his boiled eggs hard or soft.

Children should be deliberately presented with many situations in which they have to make choices. The parents *select* the situations; the children make the choices.

A young child is not asked, "What do you want for breakfast?" He is asked, "Do you want your eggs scrambled or fried? Do you want the bread toasted or not? Do you want your cereal hot or cold? Do you want orange juice or milk?"

What is conveyed to the child is that he has some responsibility for his own affairs. He is not just a recipient of orders, but a participant in decisions that shape his life. From the parent's attitudes, the child should get a clear message: We provide tea and sympathy as well as milk and cookies—choosing is your responsibility.

Eating problems in children are often created by mothers who take too great a personal interest in their children's taste buds. They nag children into eating particular vegetables, and tell them (quite unscientifically) which vegetable is most healthful for each organ of the body. It is best for the child that mother not have strong feelings about food; that she offer food of quality and taste and trust her children to eat as much or as little as their own appetite demands, provided this does not conflict with medical advice. Clearly, eating falls within the child's realm of responsibility.

CLOTHES

In buying clothes for children, it is *our* responsibility to decide what attire they need and what to budget for it. In the store, we select several samples—all acceptable to us in terms of price and style. The child will choose the one he prefers to wear. Thus even a six-year-old can have a choice in buying his socks and shirts—from among those we have selected. There are many homes in which children get no experience, and develop no skill, in buying clothes for themselves. In fact, there are adults who cannot buy a suit for themselves without having along a wife or a mother to do the choosing.

Older children, particularly, should be allowed to have clothes that are not too different from the standards acceptable to their friends. A boy with brown shoes in a class where blue suede is the standard for that year is being exposed (perhaps unnecessarily) to attack and

89

ridicule. Parents should be aware of what is considered "cool" and "square" among children. The realms of responsibility in relation to clothes can be stated as follows: We do the selecting; they do the choosing.

HOMEWORK

From the first grade on, parents' attitudes should convey that homework is *strictly* the responsibility of the child and his teacher. Parents should not nag children about homework. They should not supervise or check the homework,* except at the invitation of the children. When a parent takes over the responsibility for homework, the child lets him, and the parent is never again free of this bondage. Homework may become a weapon in the child's hands to punish, blackmail, and exploit the parents. Much misery could be avoided, and much joy added to home life, if parents would show less interest in the minute details of the child's assignments and instead convey in no uncertain terms: "Homework is your responsibility. Homework is for you what work is for us."

The value of homework in the early grades should not be overestimated. There are many fine schools that assign no homework to young

---

* The writer is well aware that this policy may be contrary to teacher's demands.

children. The pupils seem to gain just as much wisdom as those who struggle with assignments at the ages of six and seven. The main value of homework is that it gives children the experience of working on their own. To have this value, however, homework must be graded to the child's capacity, so that he may work independently with little aid from others. Direct help may only convey to the child that on his own he is helpless. Indirect help, however, may be useful. For instance, we might make sure that the child has privacy, a suitable desk, and reference books. We might also help him figure out the right time for homework, in accordance with the seasons. In the mild afternoons of spring and fall, a child's fancy will surely turn first to playing and (hopefully) then to homework. In the cold days of winter, homework must come first if there is to be TV later.

Some children like to be near an adult while working at an assignment. Perhaps it is possible to allow the use of the table in the kitchen or dining room. However, few comments should be made at this time about manners of sitting, neatness of appearance, or the care of furniture.

Some children work better when they may chew a pencil, scratch their heads, or rock a chair. Our comments and restrictions increase frustration and interfere with their mental work.

The child's homework should not be interrupted by questions and errands that can wait.

We should remain in the background giving comfort and support rather than instruction and assistance. Occasionally, we may clarify a point or explain a sentence. However, we should avoid comments such as:

"If you weren't such a scatterbrain, you would remember your assignment."

"If you only listened to the teacher you would know your homework."

Our help should be given sparingly but sympathetically. We listen rather than lecture. We show the road but expect the traveler to reach his destination on his own power.

A parent's attitude towards the school and the teacher may influence a child's attitude toward homework. If a parent habitually berates the school and belittles the teacher, the child will draw obvious conclusions.

Parents should bolster the teacher's position and support his policies regarding responsible homework.

When the teacher is strict, the parent has a wonderful opportunity to be sympathetic:

"It's not an easy year—so much work!"

"It's really tough this year."

"He sure is a strict teacher."

"I hear he demands a lot."

"I hear he is especially tough about homework. I guess there will be lots of work this year."

It is important to avoid daily flareups over homework:

"Look here, Reggie, from now on you are

going to work on your spelling every afternoon of every day—including Saturdays and Sundays. No more playing for you and no TV either."

"Roger! I am sick and tired of reminding you about homework. Daddy is going to see to it that you get down to business. We don't want illiterates in our family."

Threats and nagging are common because they make one believe that something is being done about the situation. In reality such admonitions are worse than useless. They only result in a charged atmosphere, an irritated parent, and an angry child.

Many capable children lag in their homework and underachieve in school as an unconscious rebellion against their parents' ambitions. In order to grow up and mature, each child needs to attain a sense of individuality and separateness from his mother and father. When parents are too emotionally involved with the scholastic record of the child, he experiences interference with his autonomy. If homework and high grades become diamonds in his parents' crown, the child may unconsciously prefer to bring home a crown of weeds that is at least his own. By not attaining his parents' goals, the young rebel achieves a sense of independence. Thus the need for individuality and uniqueness may push a child into failure, regardless of parental pressure and punishment. As one child said, "They can take away

93

the TV and the allowance, but they cannot take away my failing grades."

It is apparent that resistance to studying is not a simple problem that can be solved by getting either tough or lenient with children. Increased pressure may increase a child's resistance while a laissez faire attitude may convey acceptance of immaturity and irresponsibility. The solution is neither easy nor quick. Some children may need psychotherapy to resolve their struggle against their parents and to gain satisfaction in achievement, instead of underachievement.

Others may need tutoring with a psychologically oriented person. *It is imperative that the parent not do the tutoring.* Our goal is to convey to the child that he is an individual in his own right—apart from us—and responsible for his successes and failures. When the child is allowed to experience himself as an individual with self-originating needs and goals, he begins to assume responsibility for his own life and its demands.

MUSIC LESSONS

When a child plays a musical instrument, his parents will, sooner or later, hear a familiar tune: "I don't want to practice any more." To face this music with objectivity is not an easy task.

94

Some parents, remembering their own enforced music lessons, decide to spare their children such agony. To play or not to play is not their question: it is the child's. In this home the child decides whether or not to practice. He plays when he feels like it, and keeps or cancels lessons according to his desire. Except for tuition, which is still the parent's prerogative, instrument practice is seen as the child's responsibility.

Other parents, remembering with regret their own overpermissive musical experience, decide that come what may, their child will play. Even before the child is born, his musical medium has already been chosen for him. As soon as he can hold a fiddle, blow a horn, or bang a piano, he will begin to practice his predestined instrument. The child's tears and tantrums will be disregarded and his resistance overcome. The parents' message is loud and clear: "We pay—you play." Under these conditions a child may or may not achieve musical proficiency. However, the whole enterprise may be too costly. The price is too high if the results include prolonged disturbed relations between parents and child.

The main purpose of music education in childhood is to provide an effective outlet for feelings. A child's life is so full of restrictions, regulations, and frustrations that media of release become essential. Music is one of the best avenues of release: it gives sound to fury, shape to joy, and relief to tension.

Parents and teachers do not usually look

upon music education from this point of view: for the most part they look for skill in reproducing melodies. This approach inevitably involves evaluation and criticism of the child's performance and personality. Too often the results are sadly familiar: the child attempts to give up his lessons, avoid the teacher, and terminate his musical "career." In many a home a deserted fiddle, a locked piano, or a mute flute serve only as painful reminders of frustrated efforts and unfulfilled hopes.

What can parents do? The parents' job is to find a teacher who is kind and considerate—one who knows his pupils, not only his music. It is the teacher who holds the key to the child's continuous interest in music and it is he who can open or lock the doors of opportunity. The teacher's vital task is to gain a child's respect and confidence. If he fails in that, he cannot succeed in his instruction: a child does not learn to love music from a teacher whom he hates. The teacher's emotional tone has a stronger echo than his musical instrument.

To prevent avoidable trouble, teacher, parents, and child should discuss—and agree on—several basic rules. The following are examples:

1. No cancellation without notification, at least one day prior to appointment time.

2. If an appointment must be canceled, the child, not the parent, is the one to call the teacher.

3. Realistic leeway is provided in choosing the time and pace of music practice.

These rules discourage last minute "mood" cancellations, and encourage the child's sense of independence and responsibility. They also convey to the child that, while we have regard for music, we have even greater regard for his feelings and ideas.

A child should not be nagged about practicing. He should not be reminded how much the instrument cost and how hard father worked for the money. Such statements engender guilt and resentment. They do not create either musical sensitivity or interest.

Parents should refrain from prognosticating about their child's "great" musical talents. Statements such as the following are very discouraging:

"You have marvelous talents if you only used them."

"You can be another Leonard Bernstein, if you would only apply yourself."

The child may conclude that his parents' illusions can be best maintained by not putting them to the test. His motto may become: "If I don't try, I won't fail my parents."

A child is encouraged most when he knows that his difficulties are understood and appreciated.

During her third piano lesson, Roslyn, age six, had to try a new skill: to play the eight notes of an octave with both hands. The teacher demonstrated the exercise with great proficiency, saying, "See, it's easy. Now you try it." Reluctantly and clumsily, Roslyn extended her

97

fingers in a not too successful attempt to imitate her teacher. She returned home from this lesson discouraged.

At practice time mother said, "It's not easy to play eight notes with one hand. With two hands it is even more difficult." Roslyn agreed readily. At the piano she slowly picked out the right notes with the proper fingers. Mother said, "I can hear the right notes and I can see the right fingers." With obvious satisfaction, Roslyn replied, "It is pretty hard." That day she continued her practicing beyond the agreed time. During the week, she set for herself more difficult tasks and was not satisfied until she learned to play the octave blindfolded.

A child feels more encouraged by sympathetic understanding of his difficulties than by advice, praise, or ready-made instant solutions.

ALLOWANCE

In the modern home, spending money—like food and clothes—is given to a child as a matter of course, because he is a member of the family. An allowance is not a reward for good behavior nor a payment for chores. It is an educational device that has a distinct purpose: to provide experience in the use of money by exercising choices and assuming responsibilities. Therefore, oversupervision of an allowance would defeat its purpose. What is required is a general policy which stipulates the expenditures the allowance is expected to cover: carfare, lunches, school supplies, etc. As the child grows older the allowance is increased to include additional expenses and responsibilities: membership dues, the cost of entertainment and clothing accessories, etc.

Abuses of an allowance can be expected. Some children will mismananage the budget and spend too much too soon. The abuses should be discussed with the child in a businesslike manner in order to arrive at mutually agreed solutions. In repeated cases of instant spending, it may be necessary to divide the allowance and give it to the child twice or thrice a week. The allowance itself should not be used as a club over the child's head to exert pressure for achievement or obedience. It should not be withheld in times of anger, or increased arbitrarily in times of good mood.

What is a fair allowance? There is no universal answer to this question. The allowance should fit our budget. Regardless of neighborhood standards, we should not be pushed into allowing more than we can afford comfortably. If the child protests, we can tell him sincerely and sympathetically, "We wish we could give you a larger allowance but our budget is limited." This is a better approach than trying to convince the child that he does not really need more money.

Money, like power, can be easily mishandled by the inexperienced. An allowance should not be greater than the child's capacity to manage it. It is better to start with a small allowance, which can be adjusted from time to time, than to overburden the child with too much money. The allowance might be started when the child begins attending school and has learned to count money and make change. One condition is essential to an allowance: the small sum of money left after the fixed expenditures should be the child's own to save or to splurge.

FRIENDS AND PLAYMATES

Theoretically, we want our children to choose their own friends. We believe in freedom, we oppose coercion, and we know that free association is a basic right in a democracy. However, not infrequently a child brings home "friends" whom we find repugnant. We may dislike bullies and braggarts, or have difficulty tolerating runny-nosed crybabies, but unless their behavior really gnaws us, it is best to study our child's preferences and attractions before attempting to interfere with his choices.

What yardstick can we use to evaluate our child's choice of friends?

Friends should exert a beneficial and corrective influence upon each other. A child needs opportunities to associate with personalities different from, and complementary to, his own. Thus a withdrawn child needs the company of more outgoing friends, an overprotected child needs more autonomous playmates, a fearful child should be in the company of more courageous youngsters, an infantile child can benefit from the friendship of a more mature playmate. A child who relies too heavily on fantasy needs the influence of more prosaic children. An aggressive child can be checked by playmates who are strong but not belligerent. Our aim is to encourage corrective relations by exposing the child to friends with personalities different from his own.

Some associations need to be discouraged. Infantile children only feed on each other's immaturity. Belligerent children only reinforce each other's aggression. Very withdrawn children do not engage in enough social give and take. Delinquent children may reinforce each other's antisocial tendencies.

Special care must be taken to prevent children who glamorize criminal behavior from becoming dominant "friends." Because of their greater "experience" they may attain hero status in school or in the neighborhood and serve as undesirable models of identification.

It takes a delicate system of checks and balances to allow a child the responsibility of choosing his own friends while we keep the responsibility of insuring that the choice is a beneficial one.

THE CARE OF PETS

When a child promises to take care of a pet, he is merely showing good intentions, not proof of ability. A child may need, want, and love a pet, but rarely is he able to take care of it properly. The responsibility for the life of an animal cannot be the child's alone. To avoid frustration and recriminations, it is best to assume that a pet for the child means work for the parent. The child may benefit greatly from having a pet to play with and to love. He may also benefit from sharing in the care of the pet—but the responsibility for the pet's survival and welfare must remain with the adult.

FREEDOM PHRASES

A good parent, like a good teacher, is one who makes himself increasingly *dispensable* to children. He finds satisfaction in relationships that lead children to make their own choices and to use their own powers. In conversations with children, we can consciously use phrases that indicate our belief in their capacity to make wise decisions for themselves. Thus, when our inner response to a child's request is "yes," we can express it in statements designed to foster the child's independence. Here are a few ways of saying yes:

"If you want to."

"If that is really what you like."

"You decide about that."

"It is really up to you."

"It is entirely your choice."

"Whatever you decide is fine with me."

Our "yes" may be gratifying to the child, but the other statements give him the additional satisfaction of making his own decisions, and of enjoying our faith in him.

CHAPTER 5

Discipline:
permissiveness and limits

MODERN UNCERTAINTY AND ITS RESULTS

What is the difference between the approach of our grandparents and of ourselves in disciplining children? Whatever grandfather did was done with authority; whatever we do is done with hesitation. Even when in error, grandfather acted with certainty. Even when in the right, we act with doubt. Where does our uncertainty in relation to children come from? By now we have all heard about Freud, psychoanalysis, and the costly consequences of an unhappy childhood, and we are deeply concerned lest we damage our children for life. The following letter from a mother will serve as an illustration:

It is often very difficult for me to express myself verbally concerning things which affect me deeply. Perhaps I can do better

in writing. If I leave anything unsaid I
know that you will be able to read between the lines. You were very kind to
come to our church to conduct a discussion
group for parents. While it was not completely satisfactory to me because I never
learn enough on the subject of raising children, one thing that appealed to me was
your statement that you knew that no parent deliberately did things to injure their
children emotionally. Rather, they did so
unwittingly.

Not one of us willingly would do anything to cripple our children spiritually,
morally, or emotionally and yet we do just
that. I cry often inside for things I have
done and said thoughtlessly and I pray not
to repeat these transgressions. Maybe they
aren't repeated but something else just as
bad is substituted, until I am frantic for
fear that I have injured my child for life.

No one could question the sincerity and devotion of this mother. Yet she would be more
helpful if she had less guilt and more skill. To
use an analogy, we would not feel secure with a
physician who cried at the sight of a broken
arm or fainted at the sight of blood. From a
physician we expect professional competence
and some sympathy, but not emotionality and
laments. Likewise, parents can learn to deal
with children's immaturity in a semiprofession-
al manner. When handled without excessive

emotion, many discipline situations dissolve. When handled hysterically, they may become serious problems to plague the parent and the child for years to come.

PARENTAL NEEDS AND CHILD TYRANNY

A parent must like his children, but he must not have an urgent need to be liked by them every minute of the day. Those who need children in order to derive justification for their marriage or significance for their lives are at a disadvantage. Afraid of losing his love, they dare not deny anything to the child, including control of the home. Sensing their parents' hunger for love, children exploit it mercilessly. They become tyrants ruling over anxious servants.

Many children have learned how to threaten their mothers with the withdrawal of love. They use blackmail quite bluntly. They say, "I won't love you if. . . ." The tragedy is not in the child's threat, but in the fact that the parents feel threatened. Some parents are really affected by the child's words: they cry and beg the child to continue to love them, and they try to placate him by being overpermissive.

PERMISSIVENESS AND OVERPERMISSIVENESS

What is permissiveness and what is overpermissiveness? Permissiveness is an attitude of accepting the childishness of children. It means accepting that "boys will be boys," that a clean shirt on a normal child will not stay clean for long, that running rather than walking is the child's normal means of locomotion, that a tree is for climbing and a mirror is for making faces.

The essence of permissiveness is the acceptance of children as persons who have a constitutional right to have all kinds of feelings and wishes. The freedom to wish is absolute and unrestricted; all feelings and fantasies, all thoughts and wishes, all dreams and desires, regardless of content, are accepted, respected, and may be permitted expression through appropriate symbolic means. Destructive behavior is not permitted; when it occurs, the parents intervene and redirect it into verbal outlets and other symbolic channels. Permitted symbolic outlets are painting "mean" pictures, throwing darts at a target, sawing wood, boxing life-size Bobo, recording ill wishes on tape, composing caustic poems, writing murder mysteries, etc. In short, permissiveness is the acceptance of imaginary and symbolic behavior. Overpermissiveness is the allowing of undesirable acts. Permissiveness brings confidence and an increasing

110

capacity to express feelings and thoughts. Overpermissiveness brings anxiety and increasing demands for priveleges that cannot be granted.

THE NEW APPROACH: DIFFERENT HANDLING OF FEELINGS AND OF ACTS

The cornerstone of the new approach to discipline is the distinction between wishes and acts. We set limits on acts; we do not restrict wishes.

Most discipline problems consist of two parts: angry feelings and angry acts. Each part has to be handled differently. Feelings have to be identified and expressed; acts may have to be limited and redirected. At times, identification of the child's feelings may in itself be sufficient to clear the air:

MOTHER: It looks as if you are angry today.

SON: I sure am!

MOTHER: You feel kind of mean inside.

SON: You said it!

MOTHER: You are angry at someone.

SON: Yes. You.

MOTHER: Tell me about it.

SON: You didn't take me to the Little League game, but you took Steve.

MOTHER: That made you angry. I bet you said to yourself, "She loves him more than she loves me."

SON: Yes.

111

MOTHER: Sometimes you really feel that way.

SON: I sure do.

MOTHER: You know, dear, when you feel that way, come and tell me.

At other times, limits must be set. When Sam, age four, wanted to cut off his cat's tail "to see what's inside," mother accepted his scientific curiosity, but limited his action in no uncertain terms:

"I know you want to see how it looks inside. But the tail has to stay where it is. Let's see if we can find a picture to show you how it looks inside."

When mother found Ted, age five, doodling on her living-room wall, her first reaction was to pummel him. But he looked so scared that she could not bring herself to hit him. Instead she said, "No, Ted, walls are not for drawing. Paper is. Here are three sheets of paper." And mother started cleaning up the wall. Ted was so overwhelmed that he said, "I love you, mommy."

Contrast this to the handling of a similar smearing in another house: "What are you doing? What's the matter with you? Don't you know that you aren't supposed to dirty walls? Nasty child, I just don't know what to do with you. Wait, when daddy comes home I'm going to tell him about you. You'll get it."

DISCIPLINE: PAST AND PRESENT

There is a vast difference between the old and the new approach to discipline. In disciplining a child, parents used to stop undesirable acts, but ignored the urges that brought about the acts. The restrictions were set in the midst of angry argument and were often incoherent, inconsistent, and insulting. Furthermore, discipline was administered at a time when the child was least able to listen, and in words that were most likely to arouse his resistance. More often than not, the child was left with the dooming impression that not just his specific act had been criticized, but that as a person he was no good.

The modern approach helps the child both with his feelings and conduct. The parents allow the child (under conditions to be discussed later) to speak out about what he feels, but limit and direct undesirable acts. The limits are set in a manner that preserves the self-respect of the parent as well as of the child. The limits are neither arbitrary nor capricious, but educational and character-building.

The restrictions are applied without violence or excessive anger. The child's resentment of the restrictions is anticipated and understood; he is not punished additionally for not liking prohibitions.

113

Discipline, thus employed, may lead to voluntary acceptance by the child of the need to inhibit and change some of his behavior. In this sense, parental discipline may eventually lead to self-discipline. By identifying with the parents and the values they personify, the child attains inner standards for self-regulation.

THREE ZONES OF DISCIPLINE

Children need a clear definition of acceptable and unacceptable conduct. They feel more secure when they know the borders of permissible action. To use an analogy suggested by Dr. Fritz Redl, we might say that children's behavior falls into three color zones—green, yellow, and red. The green area consists of behavior that is wanted and sanctioned, the area where our "yes" is given freely and graciously. The yellow zone includes behavior that is not sanctioned but is tolerated for specific reasons. Such reasons may include:

1. *Leeway for learners.* A driver with a learner's permit is not given a ticket when he signals right and turns left. Such mistakes are tolerated for the sake of expected future improvements.

2. *Leeway for hard times.* Special stress situations—accidents, illness, moving into a new neighborhood, separation from friends, death or divorce in the family—call for additional lee-

way. We grant it because of our appreciation of hard times and new adjustments. We do not pretend that we like this behavior; in fact, our attitudes tell that this conduct is tolerated only because of exceptional circumstances.

The red zone covers conduct that cannot be tolerated at all and must be stopped. It includes behavior that endangers the health and welfare of the family or its physical and financial well-being. It also includes behavior forbidden for reason of law, ethics, or social acceptability.

It is as important to be prohibitive in the red zone as it is to be permissive in the green. When a child is allowed behavior that he knows should not be tolerated, his anxiety mounts. An eight-year-old boy who had been allowed to hang on the back of a moving bus accused his mother of not loving him: "If you really cared about me, you wouldn't have let me take that chance on getting killed."

Another child thought that his father did not have the right standards because he allowed the boy to carry a switchblade knife. Another boy lost respect for his parents because they did not stop the wild play of his friends who almost demolished his scientific laboratory. Young children have genuine difficulty in coping with their socially unacceptable impulses. The parents must be an ally in the child's struggle for control of such impulses. By setting limits, the parent offers help to the child. Besides stopping dangerous conduct, the limit also conveys a silent message: "You don't have to be afraid of your impulses. I won't let you go too far. It is safe."

TECHNIQUES OF SETTING LIMITS

In the setting of limits—as in all education—the product depends on the process. A limit should be so stated that it tells the child clearly (*a*) what constitutes unacceptable conduct; (*b*) what substitute will be accepted.

You may not throw dishes; you may throw pillows. Or in less grammatical, but more effective English: Dishes are not for throwing; pillows are for throwing. Brother is not for boxing; Bobo is for boxing.

It is preferable that a limit be total rather than partial. There is a clear distinction, for example, between splashing water and not splashing water on sister. A limit that states, "You may splash her a little, as long as you don't wet her too much," is inviting a deluge of trouble. Such a vague statement leaves the child without a clear criterion for making decisions.

A limit must be stated firmly, so that it carries only one message to the child: "This prohibition is for real. I mean business." When a parent is not sure of what to do, it is best that he do nothing but think and clarify his own attitudes. In setting limits, he who hesitates is lost in endless arguments. Restrictions, invoked haltingly and clumsily, become a challenge to children and evoke a battle of wills, which no one can win. A limit must be stated in a manner that is deliberately calculated to minimize resentment, and to save self-esteem. The very process of limit-setting should convey authority, not insult. It should deal with a specific event, not with a developmental history. The temptation to clean away all problems with one big sweep should be resisted. The following is an illustration of an undesirable practice:

Eight-year-old Annie went with mother to the department store. While mother made her purchase, Annie roamed around the toy counter and selected three toys she would save in case a fire broke out. When mother came back, Annie asked confidently, "Which toys can I take home?" Mother, who just spent too much money on a dress she was not sure she really wanted, blurted out, "More toys? You have more toys than you know what to do with. Everything you see, you want. It's time you learned to curb your appetite."

A minute later, mother, realizing the source of her sudden anger, tried to placate her daughter and to bribe her with ice cream. But the sorrowful look remained on Annie's face.

When a child requests something that we must deny, we can at least grant him the satisfaction of having the wish for it. Thus Annie's mother might have said:

"You *wish* you could take some toys home."

117

"I bet you *wish* you could take home the whole toy counter. But there is no budget for toys today. You can have a penny for a balloon or a piece of gum, though. Which do you choose, the balloon or the gum?"

Perhaps Annie would choose the latter, and the whole incident might be concluded with mother saying, "Annie, get your gum." Or perhaps Annie would cry. In either case, mother would stick to her decision, and to the offered choices. She may again show her understanding by mirroring her daughter's desire for toys—but the limit would be upheld. "You wish you could have the toys. You want them very much. You are showing me by crying. I know, darling, but no toys today."

There are different ways of phrasing specific limits. At times the following four-step sequence may prove effective:

1. The parent recognizes the child's wish and puts it in simple words: "You wish you could go to the movies tonight."

2. He states clearly the limits on a specific act: "But the rule in our house is 'no movies on school nights.'"

3. He points out ways in which the wish can be at least partially fulfilled: "You may go to the movies on Friday or Saturday night."

4. He helps the child to express some of the resentment that is likely to arise when restrictions are imposed:

"It is obvious that you don't like the rule."

"You wish there weren't such a rule."

118

"You wish the rule said: 'Every night is movie night.'"

"When you grow up and have your own home, you are sure going to change this rule."

It is not always necessary or feasible to phrase the limit in this pattern. At times, it is necessary to state the limit first and mirror feelings later. When a child is about to throw a stone at sister, mother should say, "Not at her, at the tree!" She will do well to deflect the child by pointing in the direction of the tree. She can then get at the feelings and suggest some harmless ways of expressing them:

"You may be as angry as you want at Sis."

"You may be furious. Inside yourself, you may hate her, but there will be no hurting."

"If you want to, you can throw stones at the tree and pretend it's your sister."

"If you want to, you can even draw her face on paper, stick it on the tree, and then throw stones; but she is not to be hurt."

Limits should be phrased in a language that does not challenge the child's self-respect. Limits are heeded better when stated succinctly and impersonally.

"No movies on school nights" arouses less resentment than "You know you can't go to the movie on school nights."

"It's bedtime" is more readily accepted than "You are too young to stay up that late. Go to bed."

"Time is up for TV today" is better than

"You have watched enough TV today, turn off the set."

"No shouting at each other" is obeyed more willingly than "You better stop shouting at him."

Limits are accepted more willingly when they point out the function of an object: "The chair is for sitting, not for standing" is better than "Don't stand on the chair." "The blocks are for playing, not for throwing" is better than either "Don't throw blocks," or, "I am sorry I can't let you throw blocks, it is too dangerous."

DISCIPLINE PROBLEMS AND PHYSICAL ACTIVITY

Many discipline problems with young children arise over restraint of physical activities. "Don't run—can't you walk like a normal boy?" "Don't jump all over." "Sit straight." "Why must you stand on one foot when you know you have two feet?" "You'll fall and break a leg."

Children's motor activities should not be overrestrained. For the sake of both mental and physical health, children need to run, jump, climb, skip, etc. Concern for the health of the furniture is understandable, but it must not supersede concern for the health of the children. Inhibition of physical activity in young children results in emotional tension which is expressed in hyperactivity and aggression.

Arranging a suitable environment for direct

discharge of energy in muscular activities is a prime—but frequently overlooked—condition for good discipline in children and for an easier life for parents.

ENFORCEMENT OF DISCIPLINE

When a parent's feelings about a restriction are crystal clear and the restriction is phrased in inoffensive language, a child will usually conform. Yet, from time to time, a child will break a rule. The question is: What is to be done when a child transgresses a stated restriction? The educational process requires that the parent adhere to his role as a kindly but firm adult. In reacting to a child who violates a limit, the parent must not become argumentative and verbose. He must not be drawn into a discussion about the fairness or unfairness of the limit. Neither should he give a long explanation for it. It is unnecessary to explain to a child why he must not hit his sister, beyond saying that "people are not for hurting," or why he must not break the window, beyond saying that "windows are not for breaking."

When a child exceeds a limit, his anxiety mounts because he expects retaliation and punishment. The parent need not increase the child's anxiety at this time. If the parent talks too much, he conveys weakness—at a time when he must convey strength. It is at times like this

121

that the child needs an adult ally to help him control his impulses without loss of face. The following example illustrates an undesirable approach to limits:

Mother: I see that you won't be satisfied until you hear me yelling. O.K. [*Loud and shrilly*] *stop it*—or I'll beat the living daylights out of you! If you throw one more thing, I'll do something drastic!

Instead of using threats and promises, mother could have expressed her very real anger more effectively:

"It makes me mad to see that!"

"It makes me angry!"

"It makes me furious!"

"These things are not for throwing! The ball is for throwing!"

In enforcing a limit, a parent must be careful not to initiate a battle of wills.

Ursula (*at the playground*): I like it here. I am not going home now. I am going to stay another hour.

Father: You say you are, but I say you are not.

Such a statement may lead to one of two results, both of them undesirable: defeat for the child or defeat for the father. A better approach is to focus on the child's desire to stay in the playground, rather than on her threat to defy authority. For instance, father could have said, "I see that you like it here. I suppose you wish you could stay much longer, even ten hours. But time is up for today. Now we must go."

If after a minute or two Ursula is still persistent, father may take her by the hand and lead her out of the playground. With young children, action frequently speaks louder than words.

PARENTS ARE NOT FOR KICKING

A child should never be allowed to hit his parents. Such physical attacks are harmful for both child and parent. It makes the child feel anxious and afraid of retaliation. It makes the parent feel angry and hateful. The prohibition against hitting is necessary to spare the child guilt and anxiety and to enable the parent to remain emotionally hospitable to the child.

From time to time, one witnesses degrading scenes in which a mother, to escape, say, from being kicked in the shin, suggest to her child that he hit her on the hand instead. "You may hit me a little, but you mustn't really hurt me," begged a thirty-year-old mother of a four-year-old child, stretching her arm out in his direction.

One is tempted to intervene and say, "Don't do it, lady. It is less harmful if you hit him than if he hits you."

Mother should have stopped the child's attack immediately:

"No hitting. I can never let you do that."
"If you are angry, tell it to me in words."

The limit against hitting a parent should not be modified under any circumstances. Effective upbringing is based on mutual respect between parent and child *without* the parent's abdicating the adult role. In telling the child that he may "hit but not hurt," the mother is asking him to make too fine a distinction. The child is irresistably challenged to test out the prohibition and to find out the difference between hitting playfully and hurting seriously.

SPANKING

Spanking, though in bad repute, is a popular method of influencing children. It is usually applied to child-rearing as a last resort after the more conventional weapons of threats and reasoning have failed to hit the mark. Frequently, it is not planned, but occurs in a burst of anger when we have reached the end of our endurance. For the moment, spanking seems to work: it relieves pent-up tension in the parent and makes the child obey at least for a while. And as some parents say, "It clears the air."

If spanking is so effective, why do we have such uneasy feelings about it? Somehow we cannot silence our inner doubts about the long-term effects of physical punishment. We are a little embarrassed by the use of force and we

Discipline: permissiveness and limits

keep saying to ourselves, "There ought to be a better way of solving problems."

What is wrong with spanking is the lesson it demonstrates. It teaches children undesirable methods of dealing with frustration. It dramatically tells them: "When you are angry—hit!" Instead of displaying our ingenuity by finding civilized outlets for savage feelings, we give our children a taste of the jungle.

One of the worst side effects of physical punishment is that it may interfere with the development of a child's conscience. Spanking relieves guilt too easily: the child, having paid for his misbehavior, feels free to repeat it. Children develop what Selma Fraiberg* calls a "bookkeeping approach" to misconduct: it permits them to misbehave, and thus go into debt on one side of the ledger, and pay off in weekly or monthly spanking installments. Periodically, they provoke a spanking by egging on their parents. "Sometimes they just ask for punishment," parents say.

A child who asks for punishment needs help with managing his guilt and anger, not compliance with his request. This is not an easy task: in some situations, guilt and anger can be reduced by discussing the misdeeds openly. In other situations, the child's urges need to be accepted without criticism, but limits set on his acts. The child's urges can then be directed into acceptable symbolic outlets. When the child

* See bibliography.

is given better ways of expressing guilt and anger, and when parents learn better ways of setting and enforcing limits, the need for physical punishment is diminished.

CHAPTER 6

A day in a child's life

Civilization has cast parents in the role of "killjoys" who must say no to many of the small child's greatest pleasures: no sucking of the thumb, no touching of the penis, no picking of the nose, no playing with feces, and no making of noise. To infants, civilization is cold and cruel: instead of a soft breast, it offers a hard cup; instead of instant relief and warm diapers, it offers a cold pot and the demand for self-restraint.

Some restrictions are inevitable if the child is to become a social being. However, parents should not overplay their role of policemen for civilization, lest they invite avoidable resentment and hostility.

THE "GOOD MORNING"

Mother should not be the one to wake up her school-age child every morning. The child resents a mother who disturbs his sleep and disrupts his dreams. He dreads her coming into his room and pulling off his blanket and her voice that says, "Get up. It's late." It is better for all concerned if the child is awakened by an alarm clock, rather than by what must look to him like an "alarm mother."

Yvonne, age eight, had difficulty getting out of bed in the morning. Every day she tried to stay in bed for a few endless minutes more. Mother was sweet, mother was sour, but Yvonne was persistent: slow to rise, unpleasant at breakfast, and late to school. The daily arguments left her mother tired and resentful.

The situation improved dramatically when mother gave to her daughter an unexpected gift—an electric alarm clock. In the gift box Yvonne found a note: "To Yvonne, who does not like other people to wake her too early in the morning. Now you can be your own boss. Love, Mother." Yvonne was surprised and delighted. She said, "How did you know that I don't like anyone to wake me up?" Mother smiled and said, "I figured it out."

When the alarm clock rang the next morning, mother said to Yvonne, "It is so early, hon-

ey. Why don't you sleep another few minutes?"
Yvonne jumped out of bed saying, "No. I'll be late for school."

A child who cannot wake up easily should not be called lazy; and he who does not rise and shine instantly should not be labeled "sour puss." Children who find it hard to be alert and zestful in the morning do not need ridicule. Rather than engage with them in a battle, it is best to let them enjoy another ten golden minutes of sleep or daydreams. This can be accomplished by setting the alarm clock to ring earlier. Our statements should convey empathy rather than anger or scorn or alarm over health:

"It is hard to get up this morning."

"It is such a pleasure to lie in bed and dream."

"Take another five minutes."

Such statements make the morning bright; they create a climate of warmth and intimacy. In contrast, the following statements invite cold and stormy weather:

"Get up, you lazy thing!"

"You get out of that bed this minute."

"My God, you are another Rip Van Winkle."

Such statements as:

"Why are you still in bed? Are you sick? Does anything hurt? Do you have a tummy ache? A headache? Let me see your tongue" suggest to the child that the way to receive tender care is to be sick. He may also think that mother will be disappointed if he denies having any of the maladies she so graciously lists. To

131

please mother, the child may feel obliged to admit that he feels sick.

THE RUSH HOUR

When a child is hurried, he takes his time. Most often he resists the adult's "Hurry up!" by engaging in a slowdown. What appears as inefficiency is in reality a child's very efficient weapon against the tyranny of a timetable that is not his.

Rarely should a child be told to rush. Instead, he should be given realistic time limits, and left with the challenge to be ready on time:

"The school bus will be here in ten minutes."

"The movies start at one o'clock. It is twelve-thirty now."

"Dinner will be served at seven o'clock: it is six-thirty now."

"Your guest will be here in fifteen minutes."

The intent of our brief statement is to convey to the child that we expect, and take it for granted, that he will be on time.

BREAKFAST: MEALS WITHOUT MORALS

Breakfast is not a good time for teaching children universal philosophies, moral principles, or polite manners. It is an appropriate time for conveying to children that their home has a kitchen and dining room with a pleasant atmosphere and good food.

In general, breakfast is not a good time for long conversations. Often the parent or the children are sleepy and grouchy, and arguments may easily degenerate into tantrums.

For a more detailed discussion about food, see Chapter 4, page 88.

GETTING DRESSED: THE BATTLE OF THE SHOESTRING

In some homes parents and child are entangled in a daily battle of the shoestring. Says one father, "When I see my son with shoes unlaced, I am fit to be tied. I want to know if we should force him to tie the laces, or just let him walk around sloppy. Happy as he may be, should we not teach him responsibility?"

It is best not to tie up the teaching of responsibility with the tying of shoes; it is better to avoid arguments by buying the child a pair of loafers or by tying the laces without comment. One can rest assured that sooner or later the child himself will learn to keep his shoes tied.

Children should not go to school dressed like Little Lord Fauntleroy. They should not have to worry about keeping clothes clean. The child's freedom to run, to jump, or to play ball should take precedence over neatness of clothes. When the child returns from school with a dirty shirt, mother might say, "You look like you had a busy day. If you want to change, there is another shirt in the closet." It is not helpful to tell the child how sloppy he is, how dirty he looks, and how sick and tired we are of washing and ironing his shirts. A realistic approach does not rely on a child's capacity to put cleanliness ahead of playfulness. Instead, it takes for granted that children's clothes will not stay clean for long. A dozen inexpensive and wash-and-wear shirts contribute more to mental health than do twelve sermons on cleanliness.

For further discussion about clothes, see Chapter 4, page 89.

GOING TO SCHOOL

It can be expected that in the morning rush, a child may forget to pick up his books, his glasses, his lunch box, or lunch money. It is best to hand him the missing item without adding any sermons about his forgetfulness and irresponsibility.

"Here are your glasses" is more helpful to the child than "I want to live to see the day when you remember to wear your glasses." "Here is your lunch box" is a more helpful statement than "You are so absentminded. You would forget your own head if it were not fastened on your shoulders." "Here is your lunch money" is more appreciated by the child than the sarcastic question, "And what will you buy your lunch with?"

The child should not be given a list of admonitions and warnings before leaving school. "Have a pleasant day" is a better parting phrase than the general warning, "Don't get into trouble." "I'll see you at two o'clock is more instructive to the child than "Don't go wandering off in the streets after school."

THE RETURN FROM SCHOOL

It is desirable that the mother be home to greet her child upon his return from school. Rather than asking him questions that bring worn-out answers—"How was school?" "O.K." "What did you do today?" "Nothing."—mother can make statements that convey her understanding of the trials and tribulations at school:

"You look as though you had a hard day."

"I bet you could not wait for school to end."

"You seem glad to be home."

When mother cannot be home personally to greet her returning child, a message as to her whereabouts is most helpful. Some parents of school-age children use the written message to deepen the relationship with their children. It is easier for them to express appreciation and love in writing. Some parents leave messages on a little tape recorder. The child can listen to mother's words over and over again. At any rate, such messages encourage meaningful communication between parent and child.

FATHER'S HOMECOMING

When father returns home in the evening, he needs a quiet transition period between the demands of the world and the demands of his family. Father should not be met at the door with a bombardment of complaints and requests. A ready drink, a hot shower, the daily mail, the weekly magazine, and the "no questions" period help create an oasis of tranquillity that adds greatly to the quality of family life. From early childhood, children learn that when daddy comes home, he needs a short period of calm and comfort. Dinner, on the other hand, should be conversation time. The stress should be less on food and more on food for thought. There should be few remarks on how and what the child eats, few disciplinary actions, and many examples of the old-fashioned art of conversation.

BEDTIME

In many homes bedtime is bedlam time, with the children and mother forming a mutual frustration society. Children try to stay up as late as possible, while mother wants them bedded down as soon as possible. The evenings become prime nagging time for mothers and tactical-evasion time for children.

Preschool children need mother or father to tuck them in. Bedtime can be utilized for intimate conversation with each child. Children then begin to look forward to bedtime. They like having "time alone together" with mother or father. If the parent takes pains to listen, the child will learn to share his fears, hopes, and wishes. These intimate contacts relieve the child of anxiety and lull him into pleasant sleep.

Some older children also like to be tucked in. Their wish should be respected and fulfilled. They should not be ridiculed or criticized for wanting what looks to parents like "baby stuff." Bedtime for older children should be flexible: "Bedtime is between eight and nine [or nine and ten]. You decide exactly when you want to be in bed."

It is best not to get involved in a fight when a child claims that he "forgot" to go to the bathroom or that he wants a glass of water. However, a child who keeps calling mother back to his room should be told, "I know you wish I could be with you longer. But now is my time for father." Children need to know that there are relationships and situations from which they are exluded.

NO ENTERTAINMENT LICENSE REQUIRED

In some homes, children have the power of veto over their parents' comings and goings. Parents have to get permission from several children for an evening away from home. Some mothers shun going to the movies or to the theater because of the expected curtain raiser at home.

Parents do not need permission or agreement from children on how to live their lives. If a child cries because his mother and father are going out in the evening, his fears need not be condemned, but his wishes need not be complied with. We can understand and sympathize with his desire not to be left with a baby-sitter, but it is not necessary to buy an entertainment license from him. To the weepy child we say with empathy, "I know you wish we were not going out tonight. Sometimes when we are not here, you get scared. You wish we would stay with you, but your father and I are going to enjoy a movie [or friends, or dinner, or a dance] tonight."

The content of the child's objections, pleadings or threats should be ignored. Our reply should be firm and friendly: "You wish we could stay with you, but we made arrangements to go out and enjoy an evening with each other."

138

TELEVISION: THE NAKED AND THE DEAD

No discussion of a child's day would be complete without estimating the influence of television on his values and conduct. Children like to watch TV. They prefer it to reading books, listening to music, or engaging in conversation.

For the sponsors, children are a perfect audience: they are suggestible and believe the commercials. They learn idiotic jingles with amazing facility and are only too happy to oblige the announcer by pestering their parents with silly slogans. And they ask so little of the programs: no originality is required and no art is necessary. Horses and gunmen hold their interest. So, for hours on end, day after day, children are confronted with violence and murder intermingled with jingles and advertisements.

Parents feel two ways about television. They like the fact that it keeps the children occupied and out of trouble, but they are concerned about possible harm to the children's eyes and minds. As for the effect on vision, experts assure us that there is no harm even in prolonged viewing.* However, there is less certainty about the impact of TV on personality. The experts give contradictory opinions:

* A less reassuring report, entitled "Those Tired Children," appeared in *Time* magazine (November 6, 1964,

A day in a child's life

1. Television is bad for children. It engenders a lust for violence and makes children insensitive to human suffering.

2. Television is good for children: violence acted out dramatically helps children get rid of hostile urges.

3. Television has little effect on children: personality and values are shaped by parents and peers, not by images on a screen.

On one fact all agree. Television consumes a significant part of a child's day. More of his time is spent with the TV set than with his father or mother. Even if spectacles of sex and brutality were nothing more than innocent fun, they do keep children from more constructive activities. In some homes children are allowed to view TV only on weekends. In other homes they are allowed certain times and programs, selected with the parents' approval. These parents believe that television, like medication, must be taken at prescribed times and in the right doses.

---

p. 76). Pediatricians, at two Air Force bases, were puzzled by a large group of children, ages three to twelve, who suffered from chronic fatigue, headaches, loss of sleep, upset stomachs, and vomiting. No medical reasons could be found for the symptoms. After persistent prodding of the parents it was discovered that these children were TV addicts: they watched television from three to six hours on weekdays and from six to nine hours on Saturdays and Sundays.

Treatment was radical and effective: No TV at all for a while. Where the rule was observed, symptoms disappeared; where it was ignored, symptoms remained.

An increasing number of parents feel that the choice of programs cannot be left entirely to the child. They are not willing to let murderers and thugs influence their children in their own living rooms.

Parents have a right to protect their children from exposure to daily doses of sordid sex and vivid violence. While children need not be sheltered from all tragedy, they should be protected from entertainment in which man's brutality to man is not a tragedy, but a formula.

CHAPTER 7

Jealousy

THE TRAGIC TRADITION

Jealousy between brothers has an ancient and tragic tradition. The first murder, recorded in the Old Testament, was Cain's slaying of his brother, Abel. The motive was sibling rivalry. Jacob escaped death at the hands of his brother, Esau, only by leaving home and hiding in a foreign land. And Jacob's sons were so envious of their younger brother, Joseph, that they threw him into a snake pit before changing his death sentence to life slavery and selling him to a passing caravan in the desert.

What does the Bible tell about the nature and origin of jealousy? In each of these cases, jealousy was sparked by a parental figure who showed favoritism to one of the children. Cain slew his brother after God favored Abel's gift, but not his. Esau became jealous because his mother showed preferential treatment for Jacob

145

by helping him receive his father's blessings. And Joseph was envied by his brothers because their father loved him best; he gave him a "coat of many colors" and did not discipline him when he indulged in impudent boasting.

Children like to hear and read case histories of envy and revenge. The motif fascinates them and the motives speak to their hearts. Interestingly, their sympathy is not always with the victims.

THE NOT-SO-BLESSED EVENT

In contrast to their parents, children do not question the existence of jealousy in the family. They have long known its meaning and impact. Regardless of how thoroughly they were prepared, the arrival of a new baby brought jealousy and hurt. No explanation can gracefully prepare a wife for sharing the home with a young mistress, or a primadonna for sharing the spotlight with a rising newcomer. Jealousy, envy, and rivalry will inevitably be there. To fail to anticipate them, or to be shocked at their appearance, is an ignorance that is far from bliss.

The coming of a second baby is a first-rate crisis in the life of a young child. His space orbit has suddenly changed, and he needs help in orientation and navigation. To be of help rather than to be merely sentimental, we need to know our "star" and his true sentiments.

In announcing the blessed event to a young child, it is best to avoid long explanations and false expectations, such as:

"We love you so much and you are so very wonderful that daddy and I decided to have another baby, just like you. You'll love the new baby. It will be your baby, too. You'll be proud of him. And you'll always have someone to play with."

This explanation sounds neither honest nor convincing. It is more logical for the child to conclude, "If they really loved me, they would not look for another child. I am not good enough, so they want to exchange me for a newer model."

It hurts to share mother's love. In a child's experience, sharing means getting less, like sharing an apple or a piece of gum. The prospect of sharing mother is worrisome enough, but our expectation that the child should delight in it is beyond his logic. As pregnancy proceeds, his suspicions seem more valid. He notices that even though the baby has not yet arrived, it has already occupied mother. Mother is less available to him. She may be sick in bed, or tired and resting. He cannot even sit in her lap, because it is taken by a hidden, yet ever present, intruder.

Introducing the intruder.—The coming of a baby can be announced without pomp and fanfare to a young child. It is sufficient to state,

"We are going to have a new baby in our family." Regardless of the child's immediate reaction, we will know that there are many unasked questions on his mind, and many unexpressed worries in his heart. Fortunately, as parents, we are in a good position to help our children live through these times of crisis.

Nothing can change the fact that a new baby is a threat to a child's security. However, whether his character will be enhanced or warped by the stress and strain of the crisis depends on our wisdom and skill. The following is an extreme example of a devastating introduction to a new baby:

> When John was born ... my father took me up to see him, [and] to this *day* I can remember seeing that red-faced baby in my mother's arms and hearing my father say to me: 'Now you're going to have to be extra good because we have another baby now. You are not the *only one* any more. From now on it's going to be *you and your baby brother.* Two of you, where there was only one before.' ... I think my whole life from then on was devoted to seeing if I could not outshine my brother ... and make life hell for him.*

* Virginia M. Axline, "And Hast Thou Slain the Jabberwock?" (Unpublished Ed.D. thesis, Teachers College, Columbia University, 1950), pp. 178-79.

In contrast, the following example illustrates a helpful introduction to a future sibling.

When Virginia, age five, found out that mother was pregnant, she reacted with great joy. She painted a picture of sunshine and roses about life with brother. Mother did not encourage this one-sided view of life. Instead she said:

"Sometimes he will be fun, but sometimes he will be trouble. Sometimes he will cry and be a nuisance to all of us. He'll wet the crib, make in his diapers, and he will stink. Mother will have to wash him, feed him, and take care of him. You may feel left out. You may feel jealous. You may even say to yourself, 'She does not love me any more—she loves the baby.' When you feel that way, *be sure* to come and tell me, and I'll give you extra loving, so you won't have to worry. You'll know that I love you."

Some parents would hesitate to use such an approach. They would fear putting "dangerous" ideas into a child's head. These parents can be assured that such ideas are not new to the child. Our statement cannot but do good: it reflects understanding of feelings. It immunizes against guilt and it invites intimacy and communication. A child is bound to feel anger and resentment for the new baby. It is best that he feel free to voice his anguish to us loudly, rather than languish by himself silently.

EXPRESSING JEALOUSY: WORDS OR SYMPTOMS?

When children repress their jealousy, it comes out in disguised ways in symptoms and misbehavior. Thus when a child resents his brother, but is forbidden to voice his feelings, he may dream that he pushed him out of a tenth-floor window. The dreamer may become so frightened that he may wake up screaming. He may even run to his brother's bed to check if he is still there. He may be so delighted to find him in one piece that the parents may mistake his relief for love.

A nightmare is the child's way of telling in pictures what he fears to tell in words. It is better for children to express jealousy and anger in words rather than in nightmares.

Soon after the birth of a sister, Warren, age five, had a sudden series of wheezing attacks. His parents thought that Warren was very protective of his sister and that "he loved her to death" (perhaps "to death" was an apt description). The physician could find no physical basis for Warren's asthma and he referred him to a mental health clinic, where he might learn to express jealousy and anger in words rather than in wheezes.

Some children express their jealousy in coughing and skin rashes, not in words. Others wet the bed, thus expressing with one organ what they should be able to express with another. Some children become destructive: they break plates instead of voicing their hates. Some children bite their nails or pluck their hair as a cover-up for wanting to bite and hurt their brothers and sisters. All these children need to express their feelings in words rather than in symptoms. Parents are in a key position to help children unlock their feelings.

The many faces of jealousy.—To be on the safe side, parents need to assume that jealousy exists in their own children, even though it is not visible to the naked eye. Jealousy has many faces and many disguises: it can manifest itself in constant competitiveness or in avoidance of all contests, in pushy popularity or in wallflower meekness, in reckless generosity or in ruthless greed. The bitter fruits of unresolved childhood rivalries are all around us in adult life. They can be seen in the irrational rivalry of the man who is in a perpetual race with every car on the road, or who cannot gracefully lose a ping-pong game, or who is always ready to bet his life and fortune in order to prove a point, or who needs to contribute more than others even when it is more than he can afford. They can also be seen in the man who shuns all competition, who feels defeated before a struggle begins, who is always ready to take a back seat, who does not stand up even for his legitimate rights. Thus sibling rivalry affects a child's life more than is realized. It may indelibly stamp his personality and distort his character.

151

The origins of jealousy.— Jealousy originates in an infant's desire to be his mother's only "dearly beloved." This desire is so possessive that it tolerates no rivals. When brothers and sisters arrive, the child competes with them for the *exclusive* love of both parents. The competition may be open or hidden, depending on the parents' attitudes toward jealousy. Some parents are so angered by sibling rivalry that they punish any overt sign of it. Other parents bend backward almost acrobatically to avoid giving cause for jealousy. They try to convince their children that all of them are loved equally and therefore have no reason to be jealous. Gifts, praise, vacations, favors, clothes, and food are measured and doled out with equality and justice for all.

Yet neither of these approaches brings relief from envy. Neither equal punishment nor equal praise can quench the desire for exclusive love. Since such a desire is unfulfillable, jealousy can never be totally prevented. However, whether the fire of jealousy will flicker safely or flare up dangerously depends on our attitudes and acts.

ATTITUDES THAT FOSTER JEALOUSY

Under normal conditions, age and sex differences may cause jealousy among siblings. The older brother is envied because he has more privileges and greater independence. The baby is envied because he is more protected. A girl envies her brother because he has a penis and seems to have greater freedom. A boy envies his sister because she seems to receive special attention.

Danger develops when parents, out of their own needs, give the age and sex differences preferential emphasis. When the helplessness of a baby is preferred to the independence of a six-year-old, or vice versa, jealousy will be intensified. The same is true if a child is overvalued because of his gender, looks, intelligence, musical abilities, or social skills. Superior natural endowment may cause envy, but it is the overprizing of a trait or a talent that leads to relentless rivalry among children.

It is not suggested that older and younger children should be treated alike. On the contrary, age should bring new privileges and new responsibilities. An older child will have, as a matter of course, a larger allowance, later bedtime hours, and more freedom to stay outside the home than a younger child. These privileges are granted openly and graciously so that all children will look forward to growing up.

The younger child may envy the privilege of the older one. We can help him deal with his feelings, not by explaining facts, but by understanding emotions:

"You wish you too could stay up late."

"You wish you were older."

"You wish you were not six years old, but nine years old."

"I know, but your bedtime is now."

Parents may unwittingly foster jealousy by demanding that one child make sacrifices for another:

"The baby needs your crib. You can sleep on the sofa."

"Sorry. We cannot get your new skates this year. We need the money to buy winter clothes for the baby."

The danger is that the child may feel deprived not merely of possession but also of affection. Therefore, such demands should be cushioned with affection and appreciation.

DEALING WITH JEALOUSY

The very young express their jealousy undiplomatically: they inquire whether babies ever die, suggest that "it" be sent back to the hospital or put in the garbage disposal unit. The more enterprising youngsters may even engage in military operations against the invader. They may harass him mercilessly: they may hug him boa-constrictor style and may push, punch, or pummel him whenever possible. In extreme cases, a jealous sibling can cause irreversible harm.

As parents, we cannot allow a child to bully his brother or sister. Sadistic attacks, whether physical or verbal, must be stopped because they harm both the victim and the bully. And both children need our strength and care. Fortunately, to protect the physical safety of the young child, we do not need to attack the emotional security of the older child.

When a three-year-old child is caught harassing the baby, he should be stopped promptly and his motives stated to him openly:

"You don't like the baby."

"You are angry at him."

"Show me how angry you are. I'll *watch*."

The child should be handed a large doll, upon which he is allowed to vent his anger. He may spank the doll, stick a finger in the eye, throw it on the floor and step on it.

We do not suggest to the child what to do.

Our role is to observe with a neutral eye and to respond with a sympathetic tongue: we will not be shocked by the ferocity of his feelings or at the cruelty of his attacks. The feelings are honest and the attack is harmless. It is better that his anger be vented symbolically against an inanimate object than directly against a living baby or symptomatically against himself.

Our comments should be brief and easy:

"You are showing me how angry you are!"

"Now mommy knows."

"When you get angry come and tell me."

This approach is more helpful in reducing jealousy than either punishment or insult. In contrast, the following approach is unhelpful:

When mother caught Walter, aged four, dragging his baby brother by his feet, she exploded: "What is the matter with you? You want to kill him? You want to kill your own brother? Don't you know that you can maim him for life? You want him to be a cripple? How many times have I told you not to take him out of his crib. Don't touch him, just don't touch him, ever!"

Older children, too, should be faced with their feelings of jealousy. With them it is possible to converse more openly:

"It is easy to see that you don't like the baby."

"You wish he were not here."

"You wish you were the only one."

"You wish you had me all for yourself."

"You get angry when you see me fuss with him."

"You want me to be with you."

"You were so angry that you punched the baby. I cannot ever allow you to hurt him, but you can tell me when you feel left out."

"When you feel all alone, I will make more time for you, so that you won't feel lonely inside."

Love—uniform or unique? quality or equality?—Those who want to be superfair to each child often end up being furious with all their children. Nothing is so self-defeating as measured fairness. When a mother cannot give a bigger apple or stronger hug to one child for fear of antagonizing the other, life becomes unbearable. The effort entailed in measuring either emotional or material giving can make any person tired and angry. Children do not yearn for equal shares of love: they need to be loved uniquely, not uniformly. The emphasis is on quality, not equality.

We do not love all our children the same way, and there is no need to pretend that we do. We love each child uniquely, and we do not have to labor so hard to cover it up. The more vigilant we are to prevent apparent discrimination, the more alert each child becomes, in detecting instances of seeming inequality. Unwittingly and unwillingly, we find ourselves on the defensive against the child's universal battle cry, *"No fair."*

Let us not be taken in by the children's propaganda. Let us neither claim extenuating circumstances, nor proclaim our innocence, nor disprove their charge. Let us resist the temptation to explain the situation or to defend our position. Let us not be drawn into endless arguments about the fairness or unfairness of our decisions. And above all, let us not be pushed into rationing or portioning our love for the sake of fairness.

To each child, let us convey the uniqueness of our relationship, not its fairness or sameness.

When we spend a few moments or a few hours with one of our children, let us be with him fully. For that period, let the boy feel that he is our only son and let the girl feel that she is our only daughter. When we are out with one child, let us not be preoccupied with the others; let us not talk about them or buy them presents. For the moment to be memorable, our attention must be undivided.

CHAPTER 8

Some sources of anxiety in children

Parents are aware that every child has his share of fear and anxiety. They are not aware, however, of the sources of such anxiety. Parents frequently ask, "Why is my child so fearful? He has no reason to be afraid." One father went so far as to say to his anxious child, "Stop this utter nonsense. You know you are perfectly happy."

It may be helpful to describe some of the sources of anxiety in children and to offer some ways of coping with anxiety.

ANXIETY DUE TO FEAR OF ABANDONMENT

A child's greatest fear is of being unloved and abandoned by his parents. As John Steinbeck put it so dramatically in *East of Eden:* "The greatest terror a child can have is that he is not loved, and rejection is the hell he fears. ... And with rejection comes anger, and with anger some kind of crime in revenge. . . . One child, refused the love he craves, kicks the cat and hides his secret guilt: and another steals so that money will make him loved; and a third conquers the world—and always the guilt and revenge and more guilt."

A child should never be threatened with abandonment. Neither in jest nor in anger should a child be warned that he will be deserted. One frequently overhears an exasperated mother in the street or supermarket scream at her dawdling child, "If you don't come right away, I shall leave you here." Such a statement will arouse the ever lurking fear of abandonment. It fans the flames of the fantasy of being left alone in the world. When a child dawdles beyond toleration, it is better to drag him by the hand than to threaten him with words.

Some children feel frightened if mother is not home when they return from school. Their dormant anxiety of being abandoned is momentarily awakened. As already suggested, it is helpful to leave a message as to mother's whereabouts on the bulletin board or by means of an inexpensive tape recorder. The taped messages are especially helpful for young children. The parents' calm voice and loving words enable them to bear temporary partings without excessive anxiety.

When the tides of life force us to be separated from our young children, separation must be preceded by preparation. Some parents find it hard to convey that they will be away for an operation, a vacation, or a social obligation. Fearing their child's reaction, they sneak out at night or when he is in school and leave a relative or a sitter to explain the situation.

A mother of three-year-old twins had to undergo surgery. The atmosphere at home was tense and troubled, but the children were told nothing. On the morning of hospitalization, mother, with a shopping bag in hand, pretended that she was going to the supermarket. She left the house and did not return for three weeks.

The children seemed to wilt during this time. Father's explanations were no consolation. They cried themselves to sleep every night. During the day, they spent much time at the window, waiting for mother.

Children take the stress of separation more easily if they have been prepared for the experience beforehand. Meaningful preparation requires much more than ordinary verbal explanation. It requires communication in the child's native language of toys and play.

Two weeks before entering the hospital, mother told Yvette, age three, about the pending event. Yvette showed little interest, but mother was not fooled by the lack of curiosity.

She said, "Let's play 'mother is going to the hospital.' " She produced a set of dolls (bought for this occasion) which depicted the family figures, a doctor, and a nurse. While manipulating the appropriate toys and speaking for them, mother said:

"Mommy is going to the hospital to get well. Mommy will not be home. Yvette wonders, Where is mommy? Where is mommy? But mommy is not home. She is not in the kitchen, not in the bedroom, not in the living room. Mommy is in the hospital, to see a doctor, to get well. Yvette cries, I want my mommy. I want my mommy. But mommy is in the hospital to get well. Mommy loves Yvette, and misses her. She misses her every day. She thinks about Yvette and loves her. Yvette misses mommy, too. Then mommy comes home and Yvette is glad."

The drama of separation and reunion was played out by mother and daughter over and over again. At first mother did most of the talking, but soon Yvette took over. Using the appropriate dolls, she told the doctor and nurse to take good care of mommy, to make her well, and to send her home soon.

Before mother left, Yvette asked her to repeat the play once more. Yvette supplied most of the lines and ended her performance reassuringly, "Don't worry, Mommy, I'll be here when you come back."

Before leaving, mother made several other helpful arrangements. She acquainted Yvette with the new housekeeper; she put a large photograph of herself and Yvette on the dresser, and she left a loving message on a small tape recorder. During moments of inevitable loneliness, mother's picture and spoken words reassured Yvette of the nearness of mother's love.

ANXIETY DUE TO GUILT

Wittingly and unwittingly parents arouse guilt in children. Guilt, like salt, is a useful ingredient in flavoring life, but it must never become the main course. When a child has transgressed a rule of social or moral behavior, there is a place for disapproval and guilt. However, when a child is forbidden to have negative feelings or "nasty" thoughts, he will inevitably have too much guilt and anxiety.

To prevent unnecessary guilt, parents should deal with children's transgressions the way a good mechanic deals with a car that breaks down. He does not shame the owner; he points out what has to be repaired. He doesn't blame the car's sounds or rattles or squeaks; he uses them for diagnostic purposes. He asks himself, "What is the probable source of the trouble?"

It is a great comfort for children to know inwardly that they are really free to think as they please without being in danger of losing their parents' love and approval. Statements such as the following are helpful:

"You feel one way, but I feel another way. We feel differently on the subject."

"Your opinion seems true to you. My opinion is different. I respect your view, but I have another view."

Unwittingly, parents may create guilt in children by being wordy and giving unnecessary explanations. This is expecially true of "modern" parents, who believe they must govern by consent even when the subject is intricate and the subjects immature.

Five-year-old Zachary was angry with his nursery school teacher because she had been out sick for two weeks. On the day of her return, he grabbed her hat and ran out into the yard. Both mother and teacher followed him.

The teacher said, "The hat is mine. Give it to me."

The mother said, "Zachary, you know perfectly well that the hat is not yours. If you keep the hat, Miss Marta may catch a cold and be sick again. She was sick, you know, for two weeks. Weren't you now, Miss Marta? Now, Zachary, you don't want your teacher to be sick again? Do you?"

The danger is that such an explanation may make Zachary feel responsible for, and guilty about, the teacher's sickness. The long explanation was irrelevant and harmful. All that was necessary at that moment was to retrieve the hat. A hat in the hand is better than two explanations in the yard.

Perhaps later the teacher will discuss with

Zachary his anger about her absence, and point out better ways of coping with it.

ANXIETY DUE TO DENIAL OF AUTONOMY AND STATUS

When a child is prevented from engaging in activities and assuming responsibilities for which he is ready, his inner reaction is that of resentment and anger. Anger, in turn, may lead to revenge fantasies, which bring either guilt or fear of retaliation. In either case, the result is anxiety.

Little children do not master skills with polished proficiency. They take a long time to tie their shoes, to button their coats, to put on their galoshes, to unscrew the lid of a jar, or to turn a doorknob. The best help that can be offered to them is tolerant waiting and a light comment about the difficulty of the task. "It is not easy to put on these galoshes." "The lid of this jar is hard to unscrew."

Such comments are of help to the child whether he fails or succeeds in his efforts. If he succeeds, he has the satisfaction of knowing that he managed a difficult chore. If he fails, he has the consolation that his parents knew the task was hard. In either case, the child experiences sympathy and support, which leads to greater intimacy between him and his parents. The child does not consider himself inadequate because he did not succeed in a task.

Some sources of anxiety in children

It is essential that a child's life not be ruled by the adult's need for efficiency. Efficiency is the enemy of infancy. It is too costly in terms of the child's emotional economy. It drains the child's resources, prevents growth, stifles interests, and may lead to emotional bankruptcy.

ANXIETY DUE TO FRICTION BETWEEN PARENTS

When parents fight, children feel anxious and guilty—anxious because their home is threatened, guilty because of their actual or imagined role in the family friction. Justifiably or not, children assume that they are the cause of domestic strife.

Children do not remain neutral in the civil war between the states of mind. They side either with father or with mother. The consequences are harmful to both their psychosexual and character development. When a boy rejects his father or a girl her mother, the children remain without a proper model of identification. Rejection is expressed by an aversion for identifying with traits, for emulating values, and for imitating conduct. In extreme cases, such rejection may result in a confused sexual identification, and an inability to live out one's biological destiny. When a boy rejects his mother or a girl her father, the child may grow up suspicious of, and hostile to, all persons of the opposite sex.

168

Some sources of anxiety in children

When parents are forced to compete for their children's affection, they frequently use unpedagogic means, such as bribery, flattery, and lies. The children grow up with divided loyalties and abiding ambivalence. Furthermore, the need to protect one parent from the other and the opportunity to play one parent against the other leave a permanent mark on children's character. From early childhood, they become aware of their inflated worth to the bidding rivals, and they put an ever increasing price on themselves. They learn to manipulate and exploit, to plot and blackmail, to spy and gossip. They learn to live in a world where integrity is a liability and honesty a hindrance; a world which fosters and rewards psychopathic behavior.

ANXIETY DUE TO INTERFERENCE WITH PHYSICAL ACTIVITY

In many modern homes, young children are frustrated by a lack of space for motor activity. Cramped apartments and costly furniture result in strict inhibition of climbing, running, and jumping. The restrictions usually start very early in the child's life. The infant may not be allowed to stand in his carriage, the toddler to climb stairs, or the baby to run around the living room.

Children, so frustrated, store up tension that creates anxiety. The solution is indicated in the

169

description of the problem. Young children need to release their tension in physical activity. They need space to run and adequate materials for play. They need a room or a yard that permits assertive activity within a setting of psychological security.

ANXIETY DUE TO LIFE'S END

To adults, the tragedy of death lies in its irreversibility. Death, so final and eternal, is the end of all hope. Therefore death is personally inconceivable; no one can imagine his own cessation, the dissolution of his own self. The self consists of memories and hopes, of a past and a future, and a person cannot see himself without a future. The consolation that faith brings is precisely in this realm. It offers man a future, so he may live and die in peace.

If death is a riddle to adults, to children it is an enigma veiled in mystery. The young child cannot comprehend that death is permanent; that neither his parents nor his prayers can bring back the departed. The futility of his magic wishes in the face of death is a severe blow to the child. It shakes his belief in his power to influence events by wishful thinking, and it makes him feel weak and anxious. What the child sees is that in spite of his tears and protests, a beloved pet or person is no longer with him. Consequently he feels abandoned

170

and unloved. His fear is reflected in the question often asked of a parent: "After you die, will you still love me?"

Some parents try to protect their child from the experience of pain and grief inherent in the loss of someone he loved. If his goldfish or turtle dies, they hurry to replace it with a new one, hoping that the child will not notice the difference. If his cat or dog dies, they rush to offer the grieving child a prettier and costlier substitute.

What lessons does the child learn from these early experiences of sudden loss and quick replacement? He may conclude that the loss of loved ones is of no great importance; that love may easily be transferred and loyalty easily shifted.

A child should not be deprived of his right to grieve and to mourn. He should be free to feel sorrow in the loss of someone loved. The child's humanity is deepened, and his character ennobled, when he can lament the end of life and love.

The basic premise is that children should not be excluded from sharing the sorrows as well as the joys that inevitably arise in the course of family life. When a death occurs and the child is not told what happened, he may remain shrouded in nameless anxiety. Or he may fill the gap in his knowledge with fearful and confused explanations of his own. He may blame himself for the loss and feel separated not only from the dead, but also from the living.

Some sources of anxiety in children

The first step in helping children face their loss is to allow them to express fully their fears, fantasies, and feelings. Comfort and consolation come from sharing deep emotions with a listener who cares. The parents may also put into words some of the feelings that a child is bound to have, but may find difficult to express. For example, after the death of a grandmother to whom the child was attached, a parent might say:

"You miss grandma."

"You miss her a lot."

"You loved her so much."

"And she loved you."

"You wish she were with us."

"You wish she were still alive."

"It is hard to believe that she died."

"It is hard to believe that she is no longer with us."

"You remember her so well."

Such statements convey to the child his parent's interest in his feelings and thoughts, and encourage him to share his fears and fantasies. He may want to know whether dying hurts, whether the dead ever come back, whether he and his parents will ever die. The answers should be brief and truthful: when one dies the body feels no pain at all; a dead person never returns; it is natural to die when one is very old.

In talking to children about death, it is best to avoid euphemisms. When told that grandfather went to his eternal sleep, one four-year-old girl asked if he took his pajamas with him. She was also afraid that grandpa was angry at her because she had not said "good night" to him before he went to sleep.

When told that "grandmother went to heaven and became an angel," one five-year-old boy prayed that the rest of the family would die and become angels, too.

When a child is given the facts simply and honestly, accompanied by an affectionate hug and a loving look, he feels reassured. This approach is effective when the parents themselves have accepted the realities of life and death. In all matters of importance, attitudes speak louder than words.

❀ **CHAPTER 9**

Sex education

Many parents think that sex education is a conversation. "One of these days," the parent will take his preadolescent aside and tell him the "facts of life." Boys are warned of the dangers of V.D. and girls are told of the perils of pregnancy. But sex education begins before that.

Parents' own sensuality.—Sex education starts with the parents' attitudes toward their own sensuality. Do they like the sights and smells and feel of their bodies, or do they think that there is something uncouth and unesthetic about them? Do they delight in each other's naked presence, or do they close their eyes and clothe their bodies in shame? Do they have any special aversions to their own or the partner's sex, or do they appreciate it? Do they see each

177

other as inconsiderate and exploitive, or as exciting initiators of shared pleasures?

Whatever the parents' unspoken feelings are, they will be conveyed to the children, even if their spoken words tell about birds, bees, and daffodils. This is the reason why it is so difficult to tell parents precisely what to reply to a child's questions about sex. Their own bewilderment in this area must first be known and their worries and embarrassment modified.

BEGINNING OF SEXUAL FEELINGS

From birth on, infants are equipped to feel body pleasures, and from birth on, sex attitudes are in the process of forming. Though not in an adult way, the infant's enjoyment of his body and its functions is sexual in nature. As soon as he is physically able, a child explores his body. He handles his limbs and delights in being touched, tickled, and cuddled. These early touchings and strokings are part of his sex education. Through them he learns to receive love.

There was a time when mothers were warned against cuddling and playing with their babies, lest they be spoiled. Even then, this maxim did not make sense to most mothers. Mothers know instinctively that *not* playing with a baby may spoil him. Now we know that a baby needs a great deal of tender touching and of cuddly care.

When a child discovers that the mouth grants extra pleasure, anything he can move goes there: a thumb, a blanket, a toy. The sucking, chewing, and biting bring pleasant sensations even when applied to inedible objects. These mouth pleasures should not be stopped, only regulated. We must see to it that what goes into the mouth is hygienic. Some infants get all their oral pleasures in eating; others need supplemental sucking, which should be granted unstintingly. During the first year or so, the mouth is the main mirror by which the world is reflected to the child. Let it be a pleasant reflection.

When sucking needs are unfulfilled, they do not disappear. They come out in thinly or thickly disguised ways. A baby may continue sucking his thumb, a child his eraser, and an adult his cigarettes and cigars. Babies may bite all objects, children may bite their nails, and adults may make biting remarks.

SEX AND TOILET TRAINING

The organs of sex and of eliminating are so close to each other that attitudes acquired in toilet training are likely to have an effect on sexual development. During the second year of life a child becomes more focused on the pleasures of evacuation. For him there is nothing disgusting in the sight, smell, and touching of

feces. While we guide him into civilized elimination habits, special care must be taken not to
infect him with disgust toward his body and its
products. Harsh and hasty measures may make
the child feel that his body and *all* of its functions are something to dread, rather than to
enjoy.

Impatient training is self-defeating. A child is
not ready for bowel control before his second
year or for urinary control before his third
year. Accidents, of course, are expected and are
tax-exempt until his fifth year of life.

In the course of early training, children must
be led to give up the handling of body products. However, it is neither necessary nor wise
to prohibit their *desire* to do so. We can allow
children to enjoy forbidden pleasures in acceptable substitute ways. It is very helpful to children to be able to mess to their hearts' content
with sand, mud, paint, clay (brown, of
course), and water. In their subconscious, every messy substance represents the real stuff,
which brings substitute satisfaction as well as
consolation for the loss of the original pleasure.

Lack of training is also self-defeating. When
a child is left completely to his own devices, he
may continue wetting and soiling for a long
time. It may be pleasurable to the child, but
meantime he will miss the satisfactions that
come with real accomplishments. When the
child is ready, he should be told clearly and
kindly what we expect of him: "It was fun to
mess when you were a little baby. You like the

warm feeling inside your diapers, but we don't want that any more. Now we want you to do it in the potty."

During the training years, especially tender care must be taken when using enemas or rectal thermometers. Harsh or even routine treatment may so frighten children that even in adulthood they may still fear penetration.

Frequent spankings, too, may have a negative impact on sex development. Because of the proximity of the organs, a child may get sexually aroused when spanked. Or he may so enjoy the making-up that follows the punishment that he will come to seek suffering as a necessary prelude to love. There are many adult couples who seem to need a good fight before a good night.

GENITAL PLEASURES

As physical and emotional development progresses, the child finds the most pleasant body sensations in the genital area. Here, too, our attitudes should allow him to have guilt-free, pleasant body feelings. In fact, now more than ever he needs our guiding love in order to be sure that his pleasurable sensations are not emotionally harmful.

When a little girl discovers her clitoris and confides to mother that it is her "best-feeling place," it takes both faith and diplomacy not to

181

cry out "Don't touch!" Yet, in actuality, there is cause to rejoice that the child has progressed normally, so that her most pleasurable sensations now come from the genitals rather than from the anus or the mouth.

GENDER DIFFERENCES

Children do not take gender differences for granted. It is a momentous mystery to them, and they develop fantastic explanations and fears about the basic body differences. Regardless of how frank our explanations are, the child decides and sometimes even declares that everyone is entitled to a penis.

A girl may imagine that her penis was lost or was taken away as a punishment, or that it may still grow when she is better behaved or older. A boy may deduce with dread that if a girl can lose her penis, so can he. Parents must not treat such fears as funny or cute childish sayings to be repeated to others for a laugh. Such fears merit serious consideration and remedy. It is necessary to help children bring out in the open their imaginings about anatomical differences. We may say to our daughter, "Sometimes girls have scary thoughts when they see that they don't have a penis. Do you sometimes wonder about that?"

Or we may say to a son, "Sometimes boys get scared when they see that girls don't have a penis. Do you sometimes wonder about that? Sometimes a boy imagines, 'If something happened to her, it may happen to me.' But boys and girls are different from one another. They are born that way. And that is why boys become fathers and girls become mothers."

Some parents try to console little girls for their implied loss by mimimizing the basic difference between the sexes. They may say to the crying daughter, "Your brother is like you in every respect—except for his little weenie. So stop crying." One mother even suggested to her three-year-old that she make a clay penis for herself—a solution that is fraught with many future problems.

When a child discovers that there are anatomical differences between boys and girls, it is a good time to emphasize, rather than minimize, the differences:

"Yes, there is a great difference between a boy and a girl. You have a penis, you are a boy. When you grow up, you will be a father."

"You are a girl. You have a vagina. When you grow up, you will be a mother. I am glad you have noticed that girls are made one way and boys are made another way."

The message must be clear and definite, in order to prevent possible confusion in sexual identification.

ANSWERING QUESTIONS

A new preacher came to deliver his first sermon in a prairie parish, but no one showed up
except one cowhand. The preacher wondered
aloud whether or not to proceed with the services. The man replied, "I can't tell you what to
do, I'm just a cowhand. But if I came to feed
my cows and only one showed up, I'd be
darned if I wouldn't feed her." The preacher
thanked him and gave the prepared hour-long
sermon. When he finished, he asked the man if
he had liked it. The answer was: "I don't know
much about sermons. I'm just a cowhand; but if
I came to feed my cows and only one cow
showed up, I'd be darned if I would give her
the whole load."

In sex education, we must forego the temptation to dump the whole load and give too
much too soon. While there is no reason why
children's sex questions cannot be answered
frankly, the answers need not be a course in
obstetrics. They can be brief, phrased in a sentence or two, not in long paragraphs or chapters.

The right age to inform a child about sexual
matters is when he asks questions. When a two-
or three-year-old boy points to his genitals and
wonders, "What is it?" it is the right moment to
tell him. "It is your penis." Although children
may refer to the penis as a peepee, weenie, or

tinkler, the adult should call it by its rightful name.

When a child wonders where a baby comes from, we shall *not* tell him that it comes from the doctor's bag, the hospital, the supermarket, the mail-order store, or the stork. We tell him, "It grows inside a special place in mother's body." Depending on further questions, it may or may not be necessary at this time to identify the place as the uterus.

In general, from early childhood on, children should learn the names and functions of their organs and the anatomical differences between the sexes. The explanations should not involve plants and animals; we should avoid what Selma Fraiberg* calls the "agricultural fallacy." Alice Balint* tells of a boy who was taken to a farm at the time his mother was due to give birth to another child. Upon his return he said, "Look, Daddy, I know everything, but just tell me, did mommy go to the bull, or did the bull come to mommy?"

Two questions puzzle almost all preschool children: How does a baby get started and how does it get out. It is advisable to hear the child's version of creation and exile, before giving our own. His answers usually involve food and elimination. One bright child explained, "Good babies start from good food. They grow in mommy's stomach and pop out from her

* See bibliography.

belly button. Bad babies start from bad food. They come out from the B.M. place."

Our explanation should be factual but it does not need to give full account of sexual intercourse:

"When a father and a mother want to have a baby, a cell from the father's body joins a cell in the mother's body, and a baby starts to grow. When the baby is big enough it comes out through the vagina."

Sometimes a child demands to be shown the place he came from. It is best not to allow such invasion of privacy. Instead, we can draw a human figure or use a doll for demonstration.

Our answers may satisfy the child for a short while only. He may come back with the same, or with additional, questions. If a child asks again, "How is a baby born," we can give him a more detailed answer: "Father starts the baby growing in mother's body. A fluid called semen, with many tiny sperm cells, comes from father's body. One sperm cell joins one egg cell in mother's body. The joining of the two cells starts the baby."

The child's next question may be the one parents dread: "How does father's cell get into mother's." Again, we shall first ask the child for his version of the event. We shall probably hear theories of "seed planting" (daddy plants a seed into mommy), of "seed eating" (daddy tells mommy to swallow a fruit pit), of pollination (the wind makes the seeds fly into the mother), of operation (the doctor plants a seed in the mother through surgery).

The child's question can then be answered briefly: "The semen comes out from the father's penis. It fits into mother's vagina." This may be a good time to emphasize that semen is different from urine: "Urine is a body waste. Semen is a fluid that carries sperm cells."

The next question that may pop up is "When do you and daddy make babies?" This is not as snoopy a question as it sounds. And a simple answer will suffice: "Mothers and fathers choose a time when they are comfortable and alone. They love each other and want to have a baby to love." It may also be necessary to add that the getting together or mating is a personal and private event.

Some boys wish that fathers too were able to have babies. They ask, "Why doesn't the mother egg go into the father?" The explanation is offered that a woman's body has a place—the uterus—in which a baby can grow. A man's body does not. "Why?" "Because men's and women's bodies are built differently." It is desirable to assure the boys that babies also need a father to love them and protect them.

THE NAKED BODY

There are homes that resemble nudist colonies. The parents and children parade around naked, in a self-made paradise of Adams and Eves. Yet children reared in such freedom are not free of worry or guilt about the human body. The direct observations do not satisfy their curiosity, and may stir up some secret strivings that cannot be fulfilled.

Four-year-old Betsy was allowed to take showers with her father. She liked to watch him and to compliment him on his physique. But when she expressed a desire to touch his penis, father's liberalism faltered. In fact, it turned to shock.

In infancy, the sight or touch of mother's naked breast stimulates sucking responses which can easily be satisfied. In childhood, the sight of naked mom or dad may stimulate genital excitement and sexual desire that can never be fulfilled. Does it mean that we must go back to Victorian prudery? Not at all. But it does mean that we need privacy, not only for our own peace but also for the sake of the children's normal development. We may tolerate children's occasional intrusions and stares when we are showering and dressing, but we should not encourage such behavior. We shall especially be careful not to lead children to believe that we want them to explore us. When children are allowed to be present while we sunbathe or exercise in the nude, they may imagine that they are invited not only to be there, but to do something to please us. They become overstimulated, confused, and caught in hopeless fantasy.

We recognize that children are curious about

the human body. They have had a chance to observe the differences between little boys and girls, and they have also had occasional glimpses at us. And they would like to see more of us. It is best to recognize openly their curiosity, but insist on our privacy.

"You want to know how I look, but in the bathroom I like to be alone. I'll tell you how grownups are made. You ask, and I'll answer."

This approach does not attack or block the child's curiosity; it only diverts it into more socially acceptable channels. Instead of by looking and touching, curiosity will now be expressed by words.

BEDS AND BEDROOMS

It is definitely undesirable for children to share beds or bedrooms with their parents. Children see and hear more than we imagine. Even if they cannot understand what goes on, the sights and the sounds are retained in fantasy and may reappear incognito in fears and nightmares. The danger is clear: children are neither deaf nor blind, not even when they are, or seem to be, asleep.

Architecturally, our homes are antisex. Few modern houses or apartments have deliberate safeguards for sexual privacy. The walls are thin, and the children are near. It is a sad

189

comment on our civilization that the sounds of
legitimate love must be so low.

THE HOPELESS ROMANCE

There comes a time in every boy's life (between three and five) when he wants mother
all for himself. She is his first love, and he can
stand for no one else to "date" her. The girl,
too, declares her love for father—a love so possessive that it tolerates no rival. It is essential
that this desperate love not be encouraged by
words or deeds. Even in jest, a boy should not
be called by mother, "My strong man," or "My
little lover." Nor should the daughter be addressed in such fashion by the father.

These are the very roles that the children
wish they could assume in life, roles which they
must give up—and the sooner the better. We
should not increase their frustration by letting
them hope hopelessly. Indulgence by parents
and nurses (kisses on the mouth, caressing of
genitals) is pleasurable to the child, but it
brings him guilt rather than contentment. Sen-
sual indulgence, either tactual or verbal, ties
the child erotically to his parents and blocks
normal development of sex and love.

MASTURBATION: SELF-GRATIFICATION
OR SELF-ABUSE?

Childhood masturbation may bring comfort to children, but it certainly causes conflicts to parents. Children may find in it self-love when lonely, self-employment when bored, and self-consolation when rejected. To parents, it brings vague anxiety and obvious concern. The sight of her five-year-old walking around holding his penis in public arouses embarrassment and anguish even in the most progressive mother. Of course, parents have heard, read, or even experienced that masturbation is harmless; that it does not cause insanity, sterility, impotence, or any of a dozen other plagues. But the assurance itself produces anxiety. One would not readily buy food that lists poisons that it does *not* contain, or trust a person who lists offenses he does not commit.

Intellectually, parents recognize that masturbation may be a phase in the development of normal sexuality. Emotionally, it is hard to accept. And perhaps parents are not altogether wrong in not sanctioning masturbation.

Self-gratification may make the child less accessible to the influence of parents and peers. When he takes this short cut to satisfaction, he does not have to depend on pleasing anyone but himself. Without much effort, and without help from others, he has the whole world at his

191

command and its pleasures in his hand. There is more than a grain of truth in the saying, "What's wrong with masturbation is that one does not meet interesting people this way."

Persistent masturbation may become a too ready consolation for mishaps and failures and a too easy substitute for efforts and accomplishments.

Children's entry into civilization hinges on their willingness to delay or give up immediate gratification for the more lasting satisfaction of parental and (later) social approval. Parental love and care not only fulfill but also create needs in children, needs for affection and acceptance. Therefore children who have known love are more willing to modify behavior in exchange for, and in anticipation of, the familiar feelings and favors.

Parents may exert a mild pressure against self-indulgence, not because it is pathological, but because it is not progressive; it does not result in social relationships or personal growth. The pressure must be mild or it will backfire in wild explosions. The solution lies in so involving the infant with our love, and the child with our affection and interest in the outside world, that self-gratification will not remain his only means of satisfaction. The child's main satisfactions should come from personal relationships and achievements. When this is so, occasional self-gratification is not a problem. It is just an additional solution.

FORBIDDEN GAMES: DEALING WITH SEX PLAY

Infants like to investigate their bodies and children to explore each other. This thirst for knowledge is not easily quenched. The difference in anatomy baffles children and challenges them to find out again and again that nothing is wrong with their own equipment.

Even when the facts are explained and the feelings understood, children may go on with mutual exploration and excitation. They invent games, such as playing doctor or house, that give legitimacy to their quest. They may also negotiate and arrange peeping games. The more daring may take on more advanced experiments. By mutual consent, they may engage in genital manipulation and may even attempt intercourse.

Parents are at a loss in dealing with these embarrassing events. They exaggerate the future consequences of the present acts and fear the possibility of sex maniacs growing up right in their own backyards.

Even sexually enlightened parents find it difficult to cope unemotionally with such situations. They may refrain from spanking or shaming the child, but they are not sure how to set a positive limit on such activities. In our day and age some parents even wonder if they should interfere in such intimate affairs, for fear of harming their offspring's future sex life.

What is wrong with secret sex play? It burdens the child with guilt, but it does not satisfy his needs. When a two- or three-year-old girl watches with wonder how a little boy urinates, it is considered par for the course in anatomy. In nursery school, where children share the same toilets, curiosity can be satisfied by direct observation. However, by the first grade, a child is presumed to have seen enough. A lingering need to peep and inspect can no longer be attributed to sheer curiosity about gender differences. The urgency of the need and the persistence of the practice indicate that the child is anxious and needs help, rather than permission to indulge. Furthermore, his true needs can never be satisfied by looking and touching, just as the alcoholic's needs cannot be fulfilled by drinking. A peeping Tom, Dick, or Harriet needs, first and foremost, limits on such behavior—limits set and enforced with kindness and justice.

When a parent finds a boy and a girl with pants down and dress up, he should not ask them, "What are you doing?" (It may be too embarrassing if the child replies with the whole truth.) The children should not be shamed or berated. On the other hand, they should not be provided with an easy excuse or a false alibi, such as: "Don't you think it is too cold to walk around naked in the wind?"

The children should be told to get dressed

and find something else to play with. When the guest has left, the incident should be discussed frankly. Without threats and sermons, the child should be told in plain English: "You and Penny were undressing each other. This is not allowed. You were also touching her vagina. This is not allowed. Little children do it because they wonder why a boy has a penis and a girl doesn't. If you wonder about it, ask us and we'll help you figure things out. But no undressing."

Our calm unblaming attitude makes it possible to limit sexual experimentation without harming the child's interest in sex and love.

DIRTY WORDS

No parent really wants his child to be naive about dirty words used by his peers. These words are so vigorous, expressive, and forbidden that they make the children feel big and important. When children use a string of dirty words in a secret council, they feel as though they have just composed their declaration of independence.

Four-letter words have a place that must be delineated and defined for the child. Parents should express their feelings on the subject frankly:

Father can say, "Not around ladies, George. That's man to man talk."

Mother can say, "I don't like them at all, but I know boys use them. I prefer not to hear them. Spare them for the locker room. In our home they are forbidden."

Again, we recognize and respect the child's wishes and feelings, but set limits and redirect his actions.

Sexual role and social function

IDENTIFICATION AND BIOLOGICAL DESTINY

To fulfill their biological destiny, boys must identify with their fathers and girls with their mothers. Identification is the crucial process whereby boys become men and girls women. Identification is facilitated when relationships with children are based on respect and love. By winning our children's affection, we also win their wish to emulate our respective sexual roles. Yet parents themselves are not entirely clear as to what their roles entail.

Patterns of mothering and fathering.—In many societies the function of the mother is more clearly defined than that of the father. To be mothered means to be nursed, diapered, cuddled, loved, played with, smiled at, talked to, and cared for. The need for maternal care is biologically determined. Lack of mothering endangers the infant's mental health and threatens his very survival. In contrast, fathering involves less nature and more culture. Biologically speaking, father's contribution begins and ends before the child is born. All other fathering activities are socially determined. Thus, in some societies, fathers take an interest only in sons. Daughters are not even acknowledged. In other societies, the father maintains the role of a tolerant teacher, and child-rearing is left entirely to the mother. In still other societies, the father rules his children like an absolute monarch.

In our society, the titular head of the family is the father, but his role and status are often uncertain and ill-defined. Some authorities maintain that the American father is mainly an absentee provider; he rushes out in the morning, disappears for the day, and returns tired at night. On weekends, if he does not play golf, he watches television or mows the lawn. Children have little opportunity to participate with their fathers in meaningful activities and conversations.

As a result, mother is the dominant figure in the family, and the chief, if not sole, disciplinarian. Such a position jeopardizes mother's age-old role. In former times, mother represented love and sympathy, while father personified discipline and morality. The children, especially the boys, derived their conscience mainly from him. It was the internalized image of the father that warned them against temptations and scolded them for transgressions.

Thus, father served as a link between the family and the world.

In the modern family, the roles of mother and father are no longer distinct. Many women work outside the home in the "man's world," and many men find themselves involved in mothering activities, such as feeding, diapering, and bathing the baby.

Though some men welcome these new opportunities for closer contact with their infants, there is the danger that the baby may end up with two mothers, rather than with a mother and a father.

THE ROLE OF THE FATHER

A child needs a father who accepts his role. Masculinity cannot be acquired by a formal course of study. It may be learned in the course of daily life from a father who serves as a model. Freud stated, "There is not any need in childhood as strong as that for a father's protection." From his infancy, the child needs to be aware that he has a father who can protect him from danger.

Three danger areas in particular require a father's guiding presence. The child needs protection against threats from the outer world, against fears from the inner world, and against overprotection by mother. The outside world is a dangerous place for a young child. Simply to survive, he needs protection against the hazards of modern gadgets in the home and the old-fashioned bullies in the neighborhood. He has to learn, among other things, to cross a street without being struck by a car and to use electrical appliances without being electrocuted.

The child also needs father's help in dealing with his angry wishes and fearful fantasies. Every young boy wants his mother all for himself. Tolerating no rivals, he gets rid of his father and siblings in fantasies and dreams. The fantasies may be violent and the dreams may turn to nightmares. Since he cannot yet separate wishes from deeds, the child becomes desperately frightened. He has no way of knowing that his thoughts will not become reality. Here father's role is twofold: to view sympathetically the child's frustration, fury, and fear, and at the same time, in silent strength, convey the reassuring message, "Don't worry son, I shall not let you carry out your fearful wishes."

Some parents are not aware of the need to protect a child from his incestuous and destructive fantasies. In some homes, the parental bedroom can be invaded by the children at any time of day or night. In other homes, children abuse mother verbally or even physically in the presence of an overpermissive father. It is best that such practices not be tolerated. They cannot but bring anxiety to the child and anguish to the parent.

Just as he must defend the mother against an

abusive child, so must the father defend the child against an overprotective mother. It is not implied here that all mothers are overprotective. But some mothers enjoy babying their children far beyond infancy. It is the father's function to provide the child with love that is more than merely sheltering, but is liberating as well. While mother's love conveys to the infant that he is lovable, father's confidence tells the child that he is competent. Because of their own less inhibited upbringing, it is easier for fathers than for mothers to allow children to experiment with independence. Father's willingness to witness and sanction a child's new ventures encourages the child to grow up without undue guilt.

The context in which father imparts trust and confidence is not crucial. These attitudes can be displayed at any time and in many places. Their display does not necessarily require special skills in athletics or participation in hobbies. It does require the ability to sense children's needs and the willingness to serve as a firm guide and friendly guardian.

STANDARDS FOR BOYS AND FOR GIRLS

Both boys and girls need help in their progress toward their different biological destinies. Parents can help by not demanding the same standard of conduct from both sexes. Boys

203

should be allowed to be more boisterous both because of their greater energy and because society requires them to be more assertive.

Mothers and teachers must refrain from fostering feminine behavior in boys. Boys should not have to bear female names, or to wear restrictive clothes, or to grow girls' curls. They should not be expected to be as neat and as compliant as girls, or to have ladylike manners. The dictum that "boys will be boys" is a valid one, and it demands leeway for the discharge of energy in strenuous masculine activities.

Parents must take special care not to feminize a son because of their disappointment in not having a daughter. A nice curly-haired boy may look cute to relatives, but he is sure to be a sissy to his playmates—if he has any. Such a stigma stings deep into personality. It damages the child's image of himself and his status in the group.

Girls, too, should not be made to pay for the parent's unfulfilled longings for a child of the opposite sex. Although a girl loses less prestige by being a tomboy than a boy by being a sissy, it is important to help her find pleasure and pride in femininity. Girls need to feel that they are enjoyed and valued for being girls. Such feelings are best conveyed by a mother who likes being a woman. Both parents, however, should be aware of the need to cultivate their children's maleness or femaleness. It is appropriate for a father to compliment his daughter on her looks, dress, and feminine pursuits. It is inappropriate for him to engage her in shadow boxing and rough play, lest she conclude that father would have loved her more if she were a boy.

Family life provides ample opportunity to demonstrate to children the fundamental fact that men and women in their different roles need each other and need to take care of each other.

EDUCATION FOR MANHOOD AND WOMANHOOD

Education in maleness or femaleness starts early in life. Yet, children should not be forced to assume gender-appropriate roles too early. During preschool age, both boys and girls like to play with dolls and to engage in "mothering" activities. This is as it should be, although some fathers and mothers seem horrified at the sight of a five-year-old boy feeding a doll.

Preschool boys and girls should be allowed to use the same toys and games if they so desire. At this age no sharp line need be drawn between the play of boys and girls. Fathers should not try to make boxing champions out of four- or five-year-old boys who would rather play with a doll house. Preschool children of either sex should be able to play both feminine and masculine games without fear of disapproval.

During school years, sexual differences are

emphasized. Boys and girls are expected to develop different interests and aspirations. Boys need to achieve prestige in masculine activities and girls in feminine pursuits. Sexual identification is reinforced by provision of interests and activities that are culturally differentiated as masculine and feminine.

School years are a good period for intensifying a son's relationship with father and a girl's with mother. This is the time for introducing girls to the culinary and other homemaking arts. Girls can learn to cook, bake, and prepare simple meals as well as to sew, knit and take care of the house. Miles of leeway should be granted for messiness and clumsiness. The emphasis is on the joys of homemaking, not on the sorrows of perfection. This is mother's golden hour to convey to her daughter the satisfactions of being a woman, a wife, and a mother.

Father, too, should welcome his son's readiness to relate to him, and his willingness to walk, talk, and dress like him. These imitations should not be ridiculed—they should be encouraged. Imitations of language and manner may lead to the emulation of interests and values. In their intimate contacts, father exemplifies to his son what it means to be a man in the family as well as in the community. Children derive much pride at witnessing father's skills, efforts, and dedication in situations outside the home. Spending time with father at his place of work and at civic and political activities makes them aware of the interest and pride that a man takes in his work and his community.

DIFFERENT FAMILY PATTERNS

The best models of identification are parents who respect their own and each other's sexual roles. In many subtle ways, their daily behavior conveys to their children that masculinity and femininity are valued.

In some families, children will get the message that a man's destiny is to make his mark in the world and to leave traces in time and eternity. Such an atmosphere nourishes great dreams of exploration, discovery, and accomplishment in the arts and sciences. Women, too, are expected to contribute to society in addition to raising a family. Such a view is successful if father and mother accept their different roles with satisfaction, show appreciation for each other's position, and share interest in each other's achievements.

In some homes, children will get a different message. Where the woman is bored with child-rearing and housekeeping, or where the husband does not appreciate the complexity and ingenuity entailed in being a wife and mother, the children will look down on the traditional roles of women. The girls in such homes may become competitive and feel compelled to outdo the boys, and later the men, at their own game.

Still a different message comes from a home where the sex roles are reversed. The woman is boss in word and deed. She may or may not be the main provider, but she is the last court of appeal in all matters of importance. As one husband said, "I decide the big things, whether China should be accepted into the U.N., or whether TVA should be sold to private industry. My wife decides the smaller things: what car to buy, what house to live in, what college to send the children to." The husband in such a home seems to avoid being the head of the house. He openly refers to his wife as "the boss." When his children ask him for a decision, his response usually is "Ask mother."

In such homes, children grow up with little respect or admiration for men. Both boys and girls see father through mother's eyes: a sweet, but "half-baked" boy, a good-natured blunderer, a caricature of a man.

Both sons and daughters are affected by the example of a weak father and dominant mother. The boys may try to overcompensate and to prove their masculinity by drinking, promiscuity, delinquency, or cruelty to women. Girls often duplicate in their own choice of partners the patterns of their original home and thereby continue the reversal of roles for another generation.

Sexual role and social function.—The importance of rearing sons and daughters who are individuals should not obscure the need to bring up sons who are male and daughters who are female.

In our desire for sex equality, we must not forget that some biological functions are immutable and have both social and psychological consequences. While social roles need not be narrowly patterned on the basis of sexual function, they cannot be totally divorced from it. Since the majority of women are destined to be wives and mothers, their public education and private expectations should enable them to derive deep satisfaction from these roles. Of course, individual women may decide to choose different roles: they may want to be mechanics or sailors or astronauts, or to run a business, or to run for Congress. While there should be sufficient flexibility for a person of either sex to find fulfillment in any occupational or political role, life is easier when most men and women are not engaged in mutual competition and rivalry.

CHAPTER 11

Children in need of professional help

Many children who are not seriously disturbed react with emotional upset to stressful situations or inner conflicts. They may have fears and nightmares, bite their nails, bait brothers and sisters, suffer from tics and tantrums, and act in many other symptomatic ways. Typically, they are wanted children from unbroken homes, reared by parents of good will, who may have been overprotective, overindulging, or overpowering. Such children and their parents can benefit from professional help.

Some children suffer from more serious disturbances. They are murderous in their jealousy, violent in their hostility, and relentless in their sexual preoccupation. These children need and must receive psychological help if they are to grow up to become normal and productive people.

Children in need of professional help

What follows are brief descriptions of (*a*) children who are in dire need of psychotherapy; (*b*) children who can benefit readily from psychotherapy.

CHILDREN IN URGENT NEED OF PSYCHOTHERAPY

Too intense sibling rivalry.—Children with intense hatred toward brothers and sisters need help. These are children whose jealousy pervades their whole personality and colors their whole life. They seek exclusive attention and seem intent on destroying anyone seen as a competitor. They abuse their brothers and sisters both physically and verbally and seem totally unable to share the affection of an adult, be it a parent, a teacher, or a scout leader. Neither are they able to share "worldly goods." At parties or at home, they do not hesitate to appropriate for themselves most of the ice cream, candy, cake, or toys. They would rather hide what they cannot use than share it.

Extremely competitive, they have a compelling need to excel. If they cannot win honestly, they will win dishonestly, for win they must. Competition becomes their way of life, and being ahead of others the goal of life. If the jealousy of such youngsters is not diminished in childhood, they may go through life treating people as though they were substitute siblings. They become embroiled in a competition for

214

life and death even in trifles, and they take every loss in sport or business as a crushing blow to their status. When they drive, they have to overtake other cars; when they play chess, they must win or they experience stress and failure. They may also continue consciously to hate their brothers and sisters, and seek to humiliate them throughout life. (See Chapter 7, page 150.)

Normal children, too, feel jealous of brothers and sisters, but their jealousy is neither a pervasive pattern nor a predominant trait. They may feel that their siblings receive more love and they may vie with them for affection. But when love is given, they are readily reassured. They, too, may like competition and excelling, but they can also enjoy games for the fun of playing. Moreover, they can accept defeat without much pain or strain.

Too intense interest in sex.—Some children evidence premature and persistent preoccupation with sexual matters. They dream, think and talk sex. They masturbate habitually in private or in public, and try to engage in sexual explorations with other children, including brothers and sisters. They peek and peep, and attempt to "catch" their parents in sexual relations.

These are children who have been exposed to sexual overstimulation. They may have slept in their parents' bedroom, shared a bed with brother or sister, or been fondled erotically by a deviant adult. At any rate, sex is on their mind too much and too soon. Their preoccupation

215

indicates impairment in psychosexual development. They definitely need treatment, and need it without delay.

Normal children, too, show interest in sexual matters. They may tease the opposite sex, giggle about boy friends or girl friends, or talk about getting married and having babies. They may also be pleasurably conscious of their sensuality: they may touch themselves and masturbate occasionally. However, sex activity remains only a part of their life.

Extremely modest children may also need professional help. These are children who get panicky when they are observed undressed. They are painfully self-conscious about their bodies; they are uncomfortable in classes of physical education and are mortified during a medical examination, even when the doctor is of the same sex.

Normal children may also dislike undressing for a physical examination or the gym. They may fuss and protest, but they do not panic.

Extremely aggressive children.—Very hostile children need professional help. The meaning of the hostility must be thoroughly evaluated and understood. Since hostility may stem from a variety of sources, it is necessary to find the cause of aggression in each specific case, so that treatment may be fitted to the cause and the case.

Occasionally we meet children whose aggression does not diminish with expression and whose destructiveness is not accompanied by visible guilt. Some of these children are capable of extreme cruelty without apparent anxiety or repentance. They seem to lack capacity for sympathy, and show no concern for the welfare of others. Nothing seems to impress these children. Censure and criticism have little effect on them, as though they were indifferent to what others think of them. Not even penalties and pains impel them to make amends. Such children need expert professional help.

Some children engage in aggression only on a part-time basis. The aggressive behavior occurs at home but not outside of it, or vice versa, at school but not at home. This is known as reactive hostility. The fighting, cruelty, truancy, or general destructiveness is a reaction against real or imagined mistreatment by parents. Because they feel that their parents have failed them, these children are suspicious of all grownups. They fear adults, distrust their kindliness and reject their favors. Establishing a relationship with such children is not a simple matter. Children with such a history benefit from treatment when the therapist is able to win their trust and to establish a relationship based on mutual respect.

Normal children, too, occasionally engage in destructive behavior. Much of it is due to curiosity and high energy. Some of it is due to frustration and resentment. They may destroy their own toys, from curiosity or from anger, but they are more cautious with property of other children. The normal child is not too fussy about his possessions. He may or may not put them away after playing, and he lets other children play with his toys and materials without fear of breakage. When he breaks a toy, he does not become upset. He shrugs off the incident and looks for another toy. He does not even feel compelled to tidy up the room. In fact, at the end of his play he may walk out of the room without even a backward glance at the mess he is leaving behind.

Habitual stealing.— Children with long histories of stealing need professional help. Persistent stealing is a serious symptom which often represents intense resentment against authority. Some of these children show total disregard and defiance of property rights. They engage in petty, and not so petty, pilfering whenever an opportunity presents itself. They may steal at home, school, camp, the supermarket, or from neighbors. Therapy for them may be a prolonged process; such deep hostility is not easily uprooted.

Children who steal only at home do not belong to this category. Pilfering from mother's purse may represent a bid for affection or for revenge for real or fancied mistreatment. Normal children may also be involved in occasional episodes of mild pilfering outside the home. They may take fruits and candy, or fail to return "borrowed" or "found" property. Gesell's*

* Francis L. Ilg and Louise B. Ames, *Child Behavior* (New York: Harper & Row, 1955), p. 286.

co-workers, Frances L. Ilg and Louise B. Ames, state:

> At five [a child] prefers pennies to half dollars. ... At six he responds to the beauty of some trinket and he takes it before your very eyes even though he denies it when accused. At seven his passion for pencils and erasers is so strong that he wants more and more and more within hand's reach. And by eight the loose money in the kitchen drawer is indeed a temptation, for he is beginning to know about money ... and what things it can buy. When the theft is discovered, he is punished and admonished. He probably excuses himself that he "did not mean to" and he certainly promises that he will never do it again. Another day—another theft.

However this mode of behavior is transitory and lasts only briefly. As they grow older, the children come to recognize property rights and to respect them.

Recent trauma.—Children exposed to a sudden catastrophe may develop severe symptoms, even in the absence of underlying personality disturbances. A child may react with overwhelming anxiety to a fire, a car accident, or the death of a beloved person, and he may develop dramatic symptoms.

Prompt treatment is necessary. Anxiety generated by a recent disaster is diminished when in the presence of an understanding adult, the child is able to re-enact with toys, and to tell in words, the fearful events and memories.

In her book *Children in Wartime,* Anna Freud describes the difference in reaction, between young children and adults, to the bombing of London. After a night of bombing, adults felt compelled to tell and retell their experience of fright and horror. Children who lived through the same experience seldom talked about it. Their fears and tensions came out in their play. They built houses out of blocks and dropped bombs on them. Sirens screamed, fires raged, and ambulances removed the injured and dead. For weeks on end they played out their feelings of shock and horror. Only after such prolonged symbolic re-enactment of the events were the children able to talk about their feelings and memories without fear and anxiety.

Psychotherapy provides an appropriate setting, suitable materials, and a sympathetic adult to help the child in his hour of great need. The therapist enables the child to relive, through play and words, the fearful events so that he may assimilate and master his panic and anxiety.

The atypical child.—When a young child shows many signs of bizarre behavior, a professional consultation is indicated to determine if there is severe mental disturbance. The extremely disturbed child is strikingly different from other children. He is withdrawn and insulated. He is like a stranger in his own home. He does not approach anyone and does not respond when he is approached. He is indifferent to friendliness as well as to anger. There is no change in his responses: no look of interest, no smile of pleasure, no sigh of sadness.

When separated from mother he may show apathy, impassively following anyone who takes his hand. Or he may cling to mother in extreme panic, as though separation were annihilation. Other children may cry on separation; however, their crying is diminished with cuddling and reassurance. The atypical child's crying is unmodulated and unaffected by variations in approach.

The atypical child seems oblivious to the world around him. He may remain fixed in one position or rock to and fro for long periods. His main concern is with his own body. Showing no veneer of civilization, he may masturbate openly, urinate in public, or soil himself without embarrassment. He may eat nasal mucus or smear saliva on himself and others. He makes no distinction between edible and nonedible objects, but indiscriminately mouths anything. He may swallow sand, eat clay, or fill his mouth with trash. Other children, too, experiment with eating chalk or mud, but they do not persist in it.

The atypical child may engage in repetitious activity for hours on end. He may twiddle a piece of string, open or close drawers, twist his hair, pull his ear, or stick his finger into a wall crack. With monotonous fascination he will spin a wheel, click a switch on and off, or turn a door knob back and forth. He prefers to play with blocks and beads and insists on arranging them in precisely the same patterns and sequences. He has an unusual memory for the kind, number, and location of the toys in his room, and he gets extremely upset when they are misplaced or broken. His tears and tantrums may stop abruptly when things are restored to their former condition.

An atypical child may display strange reactions to physical pain. He may indulge in serious self-injury without a word of complaint; he may bang his head against the wall, squeeze his finger in a door, sit on a hot radiator, or cut his hand until it bleeds. His only reaction to his pain may be queer grinning or hollow laughter. Any attempt to offer sympathy will go unacknowledged.

Even when he has learned to speak, the atypical child shows no interest in communication. When he talks, he uses phrases that are irrelevant to the situation. When directly questioned, he may respond with parrot-like repetition of the question. Or he may never use speech, remaining totally indifferent to all urging.

CHILDREN WHO CAN BENEFIT READILY FROM PROFESSIONAL HELP

The too-good-to-be-true's.—Some children seem too good to be real. They are obedient, orderly, and neat. They worry about mother's health, are concerned about father's business, and are eager to take care of little sister. Their whole life seems to be oriented toward pleasing their parents. They have little energy left for playing with children their own age.

In school and in the neighborhood, such children may continue with their goody-goody behavior. They will be meek and gentle and spend their time and energy in placating the teacher whom they fear. They may bring her the proverbial apple, draw pictures for her, or volunteer to clean up the board. From the first day on, they may tell the teacher how nice a person she is and how much they love her. The compliments and declarations of love cannot be taken at face value. These children may use the same words to a stranger or to the class bully. The sweet talk may be their way of revealing how afraid they are of their own hostile impulses and of consequent retaliation from others.

A frequently noticed symptom in such children is chronic fatigue. Under the goody-goody mask, many a "bad-bad" impulse is hidden. The effort of transforming hostile impulses into

angelic behavior, and the eternal vigilance required to maintain a façade, consume the life
energy of these children. No wonder they are
exhausted and weary.

Therapy provides an effective setting to modify over-good behavior. The setting encourages
children to give up slavish compliance and to
assume normal assertiveness. By observation
and experience they learn that there is no need
to be ingratiating and self-effacing. They slowly
begin to allow their impulses to gain some expression. They come to discover their own
wants, know their own feelings, and establish
their own identity.

Immature children.—Under this heading are
included children who are wanted and loved as
babies, but not as growing individuals who
have ideas and needs of their own. These over-
indulged, overprotected children are un-
prepared for the realities of life outside the
family shelter. They have little opportunity to
develop appreciation for the needs and feelings
of others, and they find it difficult to share possessions or to delay gratification. They are
spoiled and want what they want when they
want it. They show excessive dependence upon
parents, siblings, and playmates, and they an-
noy everyone with their constant demand for
attention, assistance, and approval. Instead of
exerting their own efforts, they want to be
served. They may demand to be dressed,
waited on, and fed. Children who remain infants are constantly involved in conflicts. They

create tension at home, turmoil in school, and quarrels in the neighborhood.

Psychotherapy in carefully selected groups is of particular value to immature children. The group offers motivation and support for growing up, as well as a safe arena for the trying out of new patterns of behavior. In the group they learn what aspects of their behavior are socially unacceptable, and what behavior is expected. As a result, they make an effort to adjust to the standards of their peers. In the group they learn a variety of essential social techniques, such as sharing materials and activities and the attention of a friendly adult. They learn to compete and to cooperate, to fight and to settle fights, to bargain and to compromise. These techniques prepare such children to deal with their contemporaries on an equal footing.

Withdrawn children.—These children can be described as shy, timid, submissive, isolated, inhibited, silent, and meek. They have difficulty expressing ordinary feelings of affection and aggression, have few friends, and avoid social games and play. They are extremely ill at ease in all interpersonal situations, and they avoid meeting people and making friends. They always want others to make the first friendly overture and even then they may not respond in kind.

Withdrawn children find it difficult to relate to the teacher in school or to classmates in the yard. They are mortified when called upon to read aloud or to answer a question. They may respond with a yes or a no answer, or not at all. They spend many a day sitting silently and staring into space. On the playground, too, they are loners. They wander aimlessly around. When they do play, they choose a quiet and safe activity that does not demand social give and take. When social contact is forced on them their anxiety may mount to the point of panic.

Withdrawn children can be helped in psychotherapy. The friendly adult, the enchanting materials, and the selected group members make it difficult for them to stay within their shells. The setting accelerates emergence from isolation and encourages freedom in play and conversation with other children.

Fearful children.—Like ham and eggs, little children and fears, go together. In one study, it was found that for more than 90 per cent of the children, specific fears were reported at least once. Dogs were the main fear of three-year-olds; darkness, of four-year-olds. These fears declined with age, disappearing almost completely by the age of eight. Other fears reported by normal children were of fire engines, sirens, earthquakes, kidnaping, fast driving, snakes, and high places. Some of the children showed slight apprehension, but did not withdraw from the situation if a parent was around. Others felt greater discomfort; they wanted a light left on at night or showed tension when a fire engine passed by or a burglary was mentioned.

Some fearful children require professional

help. These are children with persistent and intense fears. The intensity of their reaction is the telling clue. They are paralyzed and incapacitated by their anxiety even if the fear is obviously irrational; the sky may fall down, lightning may strike the house, the whole family may be swept away by a flood. There is no end to their kaleidoscope of feared objects and people.

Some of the children are compulsively clean; their whole world seems dirty to them, and they are careful not to become contaminated. They fear any speck of dust on their hands or clothes and become distressed if they cannot wash it off immediately. Other children are afraid of loud noises, high places, new people, running water, dark corners, small insects, and large animals. They try to escape anxiety by avoiding places and activities that seem threatening to them. Thus they may not go near the water, avoid climbing a ladder, or refuse to stay in a dark room.

In therapy, some of the children are likely to engage in activities that will require the fearful child to deal with his fears. They may shoot noisy cap guns, use finger paints, cover themselves with mud, or turn out the lights. The group makes it impossible for the fearful child to escape facing his problem. The therapist can then deal with the fearful reactions as they occur. He helps the child to play out and talk out his frantic fears and to lessen and master his vague anxiety.

227

Children in need of professional help

Effeminate boys.—Professional help is at times indicated for boys who come from fatherless homes or from households where there is only one boy in a family of many females. Since the identification models in such homes are almost all nonmasculine, the boys cannot help but assume some feminine roles. They may lack the characteristic aggressiveness expected of boys in our culture. They may shy away from rough games or be unable to mingle freely with other boys, and they feel more comfortable in the company of girls. Such boys usually receive rough treatment from other children. They are nicknamed, attacked, and abused. They are socially stigmatized and emotionally scarred, and they may grow up to be inadequate adults.

Such boys need professional help, which can offer to them a desirable model of identification, encourage assertiveness, and call forth the masculine components of their personalities.

Tics and mannerisms.—Some children exhibit persistent mannerisms that are annoying to parents. They squint, sniff, grimace, twitch, pick noses, rub eyes, clear throats, hunch shoulders, bite nails, suck thumbs, crack knuckles, or tap feet. The contortions and mannerisms may be so obvious and grotesque that they compel attention. The fingers may be disfigured, the skin water-logged, or the nails bitten down to the quick. And there is no escape from the discordant sounds of noses, throats, knuckles, and feet. These children need psychological consultation, as well as medical attention, to determine the necessary treatment.

Normal children may also exhibit a variety of mannerisms and tics. However, these manifestations are not persistent. They appear mostly when the child is over-fatigued, sleepy, preoccupied, or under some emotional strain.

Enuresis (wetting) and encropresis (soiling).—It is estimated that about 10 to 15 per cent of children still wet their beds after the age of four. Some of them wet also during the daytime. Most of these children never attained bladder control. Some went "dry" only to begin wetting again.

Enuresis (wetting) is usually considered an indication of emotional upset; only about 5 per cent of wetting is attributed to organic causes (to rule them out, children who wet should be seen by a physician).

By itself, enuresis does not tell the degree of emotional upset. It is found in mildly upset children and in more serious cases. Sometimes it disappears after brief psychotherapy and other times it proves hard to get rid of.

Encropresis (soiling) that persists beyond age three or four is considered a symptom of emotional difficulties when organic causes have been ruled out by a physician. Soiling is common among preschool children, but it is also found among school-age children and adolescents. The older the child, the more serious the problem. Soiling represents a form of rebellion against parental authority in general and against strict toilet training in particular. Therefore shaming and blaming a child may only bring additional conflicts and a stiffened resistance.

Enuresis and encropresis are such bothersome symptoms that even in mild cases it may be worthwhile to seek professional help. In any case, improved relations between parent and child will contribute considerably to the solution of these problems.

�֎ CHAPTER 12

Parents in need of professional help

PARENTS' CHARACTER AND
CHILDREN'S BEHAVIOR

The personality of a child is colored by the emotional atmosphere of his home. This truth seems self-evident, yet it is only recently that we have come to recognize the relation between a parent's character and a child's conduct. Some parental practices are overt and obvious; they can be observed and their influence identified. Other practices are more covert and subtle: they can only be inferred and their impact hypothesized.

Any list of undesirable attitudes and characteristics will include those of parents who are overemotional, overprotective, childish, alcoholic, seductive, rejecting, or overconscientious.

OVEREMOTIONAL PARENTS

Private attitudes and public conduct.—
Children who have overemotional parents can
be recognized easily: they are always heard
and seen. Since early life, they have learned
that they must yell to be heard, and talk fast if
they are not to be interrupted. They mirror
faithfully the turbulence of their own parents.
Frequently both children and parents are unaware of their excessive emotionality and ever-
ready explosiveness. When it is brought to their
attention, they may attribute it, not without
pride, to some ethnic characteristic or stereo-
type: "I'm a redhead, you know," or "It's my
Irish temper."

As long as they stay within their own subcul-
ture, such people are not too troublesome. But
when they come in contact with the wider community, they become a nuisance. They are argumentative and time-consuming. They are
loud talkers, but poor listeners. They are melo-
dramatic, but unaware of their unpleasant impact.

Such parents may not be psychiatrically disturbed, but they are socially disturbing. They
need some professional help to alter their private attitudes and public conduct.

234

OVERPROTECTIVE PARENTS

Relentless concern with minutiae.—Overprotectiveness essentially means a relentless concern with the minute details of a child's functioning. From birth on, such parents may worry endlessly about the child's survival. What is simple routine to most parents becomes a life-and-death decision to an overprotective mother. She is like a person who would drive a car with the hood open in order to watch the engine.

Several times a day she may check her child's breathing, or measure his food intake, or examine his bowel movement, or worry about his sleep. When he stands, she is afraid he may fall; when he runs, she fears he may get hurt; and when he has a fever, she is certain that he is near death.

Such a parent really works hard for her living. She does not stop doing unnecessary things for her child. What she can do for him, he must not do for himself, even when he is willing and able. This mother will overdress and overfeed her child; if she could, she would digest the food for him.

In short, the child's job of living and functioning is taken over by mother, and the results are disastrous. The child grows, but does not mature. Having lived, so to speak, on a borrowed ego, he has failed to develop his own. He

235

remains an infant dependent on mother. He does not know his own feelings and wishes, and lacks elementary social skills. And since mother always made up his mind for him, he has great difficulty thinking. He has little insight into himself or the world around him. He does not relate cause to effect, and is satisfied with magical explanations. Such children waste much energy in an ever-present conflict between dependence on mother and their dimly conscious wish for autonomy. Overprotective parents need professional help if their children are to become self-sufficient.

CHILDISH PARENTS

Children as playthings and as protectors.— Some women who become mothers find it hard to supply their children with a lasting, stable relationship. Though they may momentarily enjoy their infant and play with him as one plays with a toy, they cannot carry the burden of motherhood.

They themselves need motherly care and seek it from their children. In a reversal of roles, they demand service and security from their offspring. The children feel compelled to protect, entertain, and worry about mother. And since they are incapable of fulfilling such demands, they are left with perpetual feelings of failure and anxiety. They grow up deprived of childhood, guilty and self-blaming. These mothers need help in growing up.

ALCOHOLIC PARENTS

Sudden storms and periodic desertions.—The child of an alcoholic parent is exposed to incomprehensible sudden storms. He witnesses his parent change moods and behavior in an unpredictable and frightening manner. He knows that at such times nothing is as important to his parent as a bottle of scotch. He feels abandoned and helpless.

The scenes of the binges are indelible. A child sees his security symbol crumble before his eyes. He sees his father or mother dazed and disoriented, weak and wordy, tearful and tyrannical, in a world beyond his comprehension or reach. He may also be forced to cope with his parent's illness and nausea.

The alcoholic parent may love his children very much, but because of his own problems he cannot take care of them consistently. Such parents need professional help in order to cope with their difficulties.

SEDUCTIVE PARENTS

The need for mature modesty.—Some parents are not aware that their own child may look at them erotically and react to them sexually. Unwittingly, they may intensify a child's sexual urges toward them. A father who undresses in front of his daughter, or a mother who continues to bathe her school-age boys, stimulates sexual feelings and fantasies. Some parents allow their older children to sleep with them in the same bed, and indulge in excessive mutual fondling and caressing. Some parents see nothing wrong with kissing children on the mouth or in holding them in long tight embraces. Other parents use verbal equivalents of lovemaking. They address their children as though they were lovers and expect from them cavalier behavior. Some mothers love to dance with their sons. Even when dressed in a bathing suit, they do not hesitate to twist with them.

Such behavior has damaging effects on children's sexual development. Girls reared by seductive fathers have a tendency to get involved sexually with older men, while sons of seductive mothers may be flooded by erotic impulses and driven prematurely and immaturely into sexual affairs. Conversely, some may be so frightened by their parent's erotic approaches that in adult life they may shun sex altogether or seek satisfaction with members of their own sex. Seductive parents need psychotherapy.

REJECTING PARENTS

Physical abandonment and emotional desertion.—Many parents cannot even imagine a mother who really hates her baby. They are shocked at newspaper reports of children abused or abandoned by parents. The very idea of physical desertion of a child seems incredible.

In contrast, emotional desertion is more prevalent. A considerable number of parents do not provide children with the loving care essential for their growth. Emotional rejection stems from many sources, among them: immaturity, narcissism, inadequacy, and non-acceptance of sexual role.

Emotional rejection has many faces. It may appear in constant nagging and demands for perfection as well as in uninterest and detachment. It may even put on the disguise of over-concern and excessive sheltering.

Rejected children get a morbid message from their parents: "Don't bother me with your life. Grow up fast and get out." Such parents wish away their offspring's infancy and childhood so that they themselves will be rid of unpleasant chores and obligations. They feed their children with dispatch, toilet-train them in a hurry, and thrust on them responsibility for which they are not ready. Pushed into autonomy

239

prematurely, the children are dominated by fear of failure and criticism. They expect accusation and censure and are preoccupied with mustering arguments for defense. They live as though they were in a courtroom where they must justify their very existence. They are so obsessed with undoing past "sins" and evading future dangers that they do not perform well the tasks of the present.

The constant preoccupation with danger and defense is a heavy burden that leaves them emotionally exhausted and physically drained. If they are to achieve a measure of happiness, such children and their parents must receive professional help.

OVERCONSCIENTIOUS PARENTS

Happiness on a gold platter.—Many conscientious parents need guidance in bringing up children. The parents may be loving and devoted, but they are overly child-centered. They are determined *to make* their child happy even if it kills them. They strive to avoid all possible frustration in their child's life, even if in the process they themselves become frustrated and worn out.

Happiness, at best, is an illusory goal. It is not a destination; it is a manner of traveling. Happiness is not an end in itself. It is a by-product of working, playing, loving, and living.

Living, by necessity, involves delay between desire and fulfillment, between plan and realization. In other words, it involves frustration and the endurance of frustration.

We do not have to plan frustration, just as we do not have to premeditate illness. But when a child is frustrated, a parent need not go to pieces. When a child cries, it is not necessary for mother to perform somersaults to bring back his smile. Above all, children need wise management that is not based on guilt or martyrdom.

When mild demands and reasonable requests are met with tears and tantrums, it is best to insist on performance and to live through the storm. Placating a child will not clear the air. Some clouds will bring rain, regardless. All one can do is to wait for the storm to pass without getting cold feet. Children draw strength and security from our ability to remain imperturbable and sympathetic.

DIVORCED PARENTS

A semblance of cordiality.—Divorce, like amputation, is a soul-shaking experience to all involved. To parents it represents an end to many cherished dreams and aspirations. To children it may seem like the end of the world. Amidst the bitterness and confusion of a family break-up, parents must choose the course least damaging to their children.

The worst that parents can do is to use a child as a weapon of revenge against one another. The feelings are raw, the opportunity is there, and the temptation is tremendous. The other parent may be blamed and maligned, and the children may be forced or induced to take sides in virulent battles over loyalty, custody, money, education, and visits. The effect on children can be disastrous.

The best that divorced parents can do is to continue to be parents, although no longer husband and wife. It is not an easy arrangement, since it requires a semblance of cordiality amidst bitterness and enmity. Professional help may enable parents to handle their grievances more objectively and to do what is really best for their children. As Dr. J. Louise Despert states in her book *Children of Divorce:* "A man and woman may have been unable to make a success of their marriage. But they can yet make a success of divorce. With effort . . . wisdom and guidance . . . they can make of their divorce the maturing experience which their marriage has failed to be."

EPILOGUE

The new solutions offered in this book can lighten the task of parenthood only when applied selectively and appropriately. Children vary in their responses to demands. Some children are compliant; they easily accept change in routines and relationships. Others, more conservative, accept change only under protest and after prodding. Still others are more reactionary: they actively resist any "new deal" in their lives. A wise application of the new approach will not ignore the basic grain of the child's temperament and personality.

In human relations, ends depend on means, and outcome depends on process. Personality and character flourish only when methods of child-rearing are imbued with respect and sympathy. It is hoped that the new approach will create deeper sensitivity to feelings and greater responsiveness to needs in the challenging relationship between parent and child.

BIBLIOGRAPHY

Books you may find enjoyable and useful

ARNSTEIN, HELENE S. *What To Tell Your Child About Birth, Illness, Death, Divorce, and Other Family Crises.* New York: Pocket Books, 1964.

BALINT, ALICE. *The Early Years of Life: A Psychoanalytic Study.* New York: Basic Books, 1954.

BARUCH, DOROTHY W. *New Ways in Discipline.* New York: McGraw-Hill Book Co., 1949.

FRAIBERG, SELMA. *The Magic Years.* New York: Charles Scribner's Sons, 1959.

HALPERN, H. M. *A Parent's Guide to Child Psychotherapy.* New York: A. S. Barnes & Co., 1963.

SUEHSDORF, ADIE. (Ed.) *What To Tell Your Children About Sex.* New York: Pocket Books, 1959.

WOLF, ANNA, *The Parent's Manual.* New York: Popular Library, 1951.

Where to go for help

The helping agencies.—Mental health facilities vary from community to community. There are child guidance centers, mental health clinics, and family service agencies. Information about needed services (child guidance, family counseling, or adult treatment) can be obtained from local and state mental health associations, state departments of health, and the local council of social agencies.

Information about the location and qualifications of an agency can also be obtained by writing to:

The National Association for Mental Health
10 Columbus Circle, New York 19, N.Y.

The Family Service Association of America
44 East 23 Street, New York 10, N.Y.

The helping professions.—Psychologists, psychiatrists, and psychiatric social workers, function as a team in Mental Health agencies. The psychologist* (Ph.D. or Ed.D.) is a scientist with intensive training in understanding personality and its disorders. His specialties are psychotherapy, diagnostic testing,

---

* Some qualified psychologists do not have a doctorate but an M.A. A number of them are very competent "old-timers" who started practice long before the doctorate became an essential requirement.

247

and research. The psychiatrist is a physician (M.D.) with special training in diagnosis and treatment of mental disorders. In a clinic his specialties are psychotherapy, diagnosis, and prescription of drugs. The psychiatric social worker (MSW) has had his basic training in social work. His specialties are psychotherapy, initial interviewing (intake), and preparation of case histories.

The psychologist, psychiatrist, and social worker have one function in common: psychotherapy. In addition each has a function not shared by the others. The psychologist administers tests, the psychiatrist prescribes drugs, and the social worker prepares case histories.

Members of the three professions can also be found in the private practice of psychotherapy. To check on the qualifications of a particular practitioner, it is advisable to consult the directory of his main professional association. The directories are:

Directory of the American Psychological Association

Directory of the American Psychiatric Association

Directory of the National Association of Social Workers

Another member of the Mental Health professions is the psychoanalyst. He works mainly in private practice. The psychoanalyst is an expert in a special form of intensive psychotherapy called psychoanalysis. While most psychotherapists see their patients once a week, psychoanalysts see them three or four times a week. The psychoanalyst is either a psychologist or a psychiatrist. In some instances he may be a psychiatric social worker.

Index

Index

AVON  The New Leader in Paperbacks!

Bel Kaufman

UP The DOWN STAIR Case

N130 95¢

The Most Wonderful Bestseller of Our Time!

OVER 3,000,000 COPIES SOLD!

AVON BOOKS

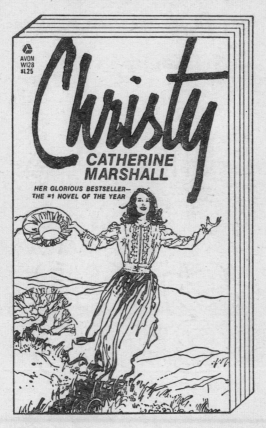